LeadingIdeas

to-the-point training

for Christian leaders

e. Nelson, ALAN Ed. D.

Flagship church resources
from Group Publishing

LeadingIdeas

to-the-point training for Christian leaders

Visit our Web site: **www.grouppublishing.com**

CREDITS
Creative Development Editor: *Paul Woods*
Chief Creative Officer: *Joani Schultz*
Editor: *Candace McMahan*
Assistant Editor: *Alison Imbriaco*
Book Designer: *Jean Bruns*
Cover Art Director: *Jeff A. Storm*
Cover Designer: *Alan Furst*
Print Production Artist: *Tracy K. Donaldson*
Production Manager: *Peggy Naylor*

LIBRARY OF CONGRESS CATALOGING-IN-PUBLICATION DATA
Nelson, Alan E.
LeadingIdeas : to-the-point training for Christian leaders / by Alan E. Nelson.
    p. cm.
    ISBN 0-7644-2448-3 (pbk. :alk. paper)
    1. Christian leadership. I. Title. II. Title: Leading ideas.
BV652.1.N39 2002
253--dc21
2002009758

10 9 8 7 6 5 4 3 2 1   12 11 10 09 08 07 06 05 04 03
Printed in the United States of America.

dedication

This book is dedicated to the
wonderful men and women whom
God calls to the sometimes fortunate
and at other times unfortunate role
of leader, influencer. May these
lessons sharpen your ax so you
can *make the chips fly*.

This book is also dedicated to Breck and
Christy Sneed, partners in ministry.

table of *contents*

leadership movies

how to use these *leader lessons*

With so many people talking, writing, and thinking about leading, you'd think we'd have more and better leaders than ever. Well, we do. The problem is that the demand is surpassing the supply. That's why leaders, really good ones, are so popular these days. Leaders address and instill change. When you don't need change, you don't need a leader. In fact, when you don't need change, you should avoid leaders because they'll mess you up.

As a leader-nut (a guy who owns nearly four hundred books about leadership and has a doctorate in the field), I'm always trying to gauge what is and isn't happening in this movement. The number one weakness I've seen is in the arena of leadership-development resources. People are looking for ways to realize the leadership potential within others. Unfortunately, just tossing someone a book isn't enough to catalyze right thinking and action in a majority of us. People are hungry for bite-sized concepts they can unpack through discussion and creative application. This is the main motivation behind *LeadingIdeas*, fifty lessons for staff and leadership teams to help them develop as leaders.

While I don't buy into the school that everyone can be a leader in the way I define the term (one who organizes others toward a common goal), I do believe that everyone can play an effective part in the leadership process—as a leader, as an influential follower, or as a committed team member. Chances are that you have people around you who are hungry for practical, substantial ideas on how they can improve their leading. By using lessons like these, you not only raise the value of your leadership team, but you also elevate the team's appreciation for you for taking the time and effort to better them as individuals. It's a win-win combination.

You have in your hands a tool that addresses a question countless people have asked me: "How can we train our leaders? Do you know of any resources?" This book is not primarily for team building. There are a number of resources on the market that can help with that. Leaders function differently than followers do, so it's difficult to address both at the same time. Leadership is a complicated process; it's not linear, sequential, or easily defined. Sometimes the best way to learn and hone leadership skills is via specific, consistent mini-lessons that address various facets of this gem. The goal is twofold: to provide specific ideas to lead better and to develop an underlying mindset for thinking like a leader.

Following are forty-five lessons that I affectionately call "leader feeders." Obviously, you can use them for your personal growth as a leader, but they are primarily designed to be used within staff meetings, board meetings, and retreats. There is no logical order to the lessons. I suggest that you select them by topic, according to the needs of your leadership team. Each lesson contains two parts. The first part consists of one or two pages for the leaders to read. You may photocopy these pages and distribute them to each participant. The second part is for you, the facilitator or trainer, and is designed to help you unpack the lesson. It contains ideas for stimulating discussion and application. Don't feel compelled to use any or all of the prompts. They are merely ideas designed to help you more effectively use the lesson to develop your team's leadership skills as well as an attitude of leadership within your organization.

In our staff and leadership meetings, I've found that a consistent twenty-minute leader lesson works best. It's long enough to provide something of substance that members can take away for application, but it's not so long that it overwhelms, bores, or frustrates agenda-driven participants. Thus, leadership development becomes an intentional part of most of our regularly scheduled staff and leadership meetings. The goal is to create an organizational culture in which perpetual learning and growth are a natural occurrence.

time and format *ideas*

■ **5-minute format**—Ask your leaders to read the lesson without discussion.

■ **10-minute format**—Ask your leaders to read the lesson and make some direct applications to your organization, perhaps encouraging a few comments from the members.

■ **15- to 20-minute format**—Read the lesson aloud, facilitate discussion, and do one or two of the suggested activities.

■ **20- to 30-minute format**—Read the lesson aloud, facilitate discussion, do one or two of the suggested activities, then add a brief brainstorming session to help your people apply what they've learned to their leadership situations.

Following the first forty-five lessons are study guides for five movies in which leadership plays an important role. The study guides will help you use these five films as effective teaching resources. While corporate training films and videos often cost hundreds or thousands of dollars, you can rent a video or DVD at your local video store at minimal expense. Take advantage of the films' multimillion-dollar budgets to capture the interest of your leadership team while dissecting the films for leadership principles. All the films may not be suitable for your situation, but some of them probably will be (viewer discretion is advised). Use this idea to design your own study guides for other films you deem appropriate.

LeadingIdeas is specifically about leadership, as opposed to management, team building, or personal growth. Leadership in the twenty-first century is different than it was even ten years ago. It tends to be more participative, less dominant, more spiritual, less academic, more character based, and less manipulative. The call today is for leaders who are more in touch with the Spirit as well as the character and souls of others.

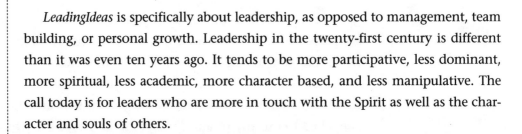

discipleship *idea*

While this book is being marketed as a resource for church leaders, the need for leadership-development materials in the corporate realm is significant, and pastors may want to recommend the book to business leaders in their congregations.

You are free to photocopy the pages marked with an "OK to photocopy" symbol for members of your immediate organization, but you may not charge a fee. If you are the leader of a large organization, you might find it helpful to purchase a book for each department and group director so they can work through the lessons in a way that's relevant to them. Our goal is to help as many people and organizations as possible improve their level of leadership and service. I appreciate Group Publishing's belief in this project and encourage you to consider Group's array of top-quality products for your church, ministry, and personal growth.

Alan E. Nelson, Ed. D.
Scottsdale, Arizona

In addition to pastoring and writing, Alan serves as a leadership coach.
You may reach him on the Web at www.leadingideas.org

the
leader
lessons

LESSON 1

NEW WINESKINS

Why learning helps leaders stay supple

Leaders who take time to contemplate themselves, their experiences, and their relationships are more apt to remain fresh and stable. Lessons learned, failures experienced, and successes gained can be building blocks toward wisdom, but we need to review them to use them. As we scurry to answer e-mails, remain current in our reading, and attend our kids' soccer games and socials, we are deprived of the moments necessary to ask the deeper questions of life. Jesus and many great leaders throughout history made it a practice to get away, to retreat. Most of us need not schedule long retreats; weekly if not daily ponderings are sufficient to stretch us.

Remaining open to learning makes us better leaders during changing times. As human beings we are always tempted to resort to the familiar, but in changing times the familiar is apt to be antiquated and irrelevant. "Neither do men pour new wine into old wineskins. If they do, the skins will burst, the wine will run out and the wineskins will be ruined. No, they pour new wine into new wineskins, and both are preserved" (Matthew 9:17). Leaders are in the new-wine business. They must remain fluid and supple themselves if they are to introduce appropriate changes to the people they serve.

The goal is not to stack up a preset number of responses to challenging situations; rather, it is to learn how to think creatively and innovatively. Old wineskins tend to be inflexible, incapable of expanding as the fermenting wine needs room to "stretch." Inflexible leaders provide diminishing benefits for churches that require both greater wisdom and increased flexibility. Farm living showed me that cows don't always take the shortest path to a pasture; they tend to take the well-worn one. Humans, too, are creatures of habit more often than they are innovators.

"Forget the former things; do not dwell on the past. See, I am doing a new thing! Now it springs up; do you not perceive it? I am making a way in the desert and streams in the wasteland" (Isaiah 43:18-19). God has new things for us in business, ministry, and life in general. Leaders must not allow emotional rigor mortis to set in.

Twenty-first century leading requires more and better leaders who possess qualities of new and old wineskins—old in that they are seasoned and mature, and new in that they are flexible and supple. Unless we stretch frequently, even the best of us are bound to burst. What new lesson have you learned in the last week or two?

LESSON 1

NEW WINESKINS

Why learning helps leaders stay supple

Context

The goal of this lesson is to remind leaders and influencers that they need to keep learning and changing in order to lead well. To remain pliable, leaders must be curious and maintain teachable attitudes. Our natural tendency is to become set in our ways and rely upon past experiences. Rigidity renders us incapable of effective leadership in times of change.

Discussion

1. What is something new you've tried in the last month (such as a restaurant, an experience, or a visit to a new town)?
2. Why do we tend to avoid new experiences?
3. What recent change has succeeded in our church? How did it evolve?
4. Identify one rut you or our church may be in, a habitual behavior or process that has not been confronted in recent weeks or months.
5. Why is innovation indicative of faith? How does adherence to the status quo require less faith?

Activity 1

Sometimes innovations emerge from problems or apparent failures.

Form groups of three or four.

Give everyone five minutes to think of and describe in writing a life or leadership lesson learned from failure. Ask participants to describe how these lessons changed how they responded to similar circumstances later.

Give members of each group ten minutes to share this information with one another.

If you have more than two groups, you might ask each to choose one story to share with the rest of the staff.

Activity 2

Try the following activity with members of your staff to impress upon them the importance of remaining observant and aware of changing conditions.

Ask everyone to find a partner, and have partners face each other for about fifteen seconds. Then instruct partners to turn around so that they're back to back. While they're turned away from each other, tell participants to change one thing about their appearance within thirty seconds. When time is up, tell partners to turn around, face each other again, and try to identify what has been changed.

Ask participants if it was easy or difficult to spot the changes. Ask them to think about how they can cultivate the habit of being observant. Ask how this habit could benefit the people they serve.

LESSON 2

HEAVYWEIGHTS

Determining how much you should oversee

Aconsultant once asked each department head within our organization to develop a flowchart for his or her area of responsibility. When the consultant returned my nice, neat flowchart, he mentioned with a smile that I might want to take a look at my *range of control*.

At first, I was a little embarrassed that I was overseeing too many departments and having my hand in too many pies, which is a typical scenario in a growth-oriented organization. But upon further consideration, I realized that I shouldn't decide my range of control merely on the number of people who answer to me. I also need to consider the quality of the departments I oversee. Just because Mike, for example, oversees several large departments does not necessarily mean that he is overwhelmed. If top-notch people are leading them, they might require very little of his energy. The key question is, How much maintenance does each responsibility require? If Mike had a few smaller departments that weighed heavy on his time and energy because of poor leadership, limited resources, lousy organization, or conflict within the team, they would occupy an inordinate share of his time and efforts.

Some suggest that leaders should have five to nine (preferably no more than seven) people answering to them. A better rule of thumb is to measure the quality of each leader and his or her department. A leader overseeing nine well-organized and well-led departments is not nearly as overwhelmed as a leader of three poorly led or poorly structured ones.

In Exodus 18, Moses' father-in-law suggested that Moses seek people capable of overseeing groups of ten, fifty, one hundred, and one thousand. The reason was that Moses was the "go-to" person for the multitudes; everyone with a dispute came to him for resolution. By identifying others with the capacity to lead groups of varying sizes, Moses could devote his energy to resolving the most difficult cases. This story demonstrates that people do not share equal capacities to lead. Some leaders can handle more than others can. By the same token, more effort and skill is required to oversee some departments than is needed for others.

Putting together a flowchart for your church is a good first step in analyzing your range of control. But realize that flowcharts can be misleading. As long as the departments you oversee are well-led and functioning properly, you may not need to redistribute areas of responsibility. If they are not running well, you may want to restructure so that you are responsible for only one to three areas. Do this analysis periodically to respond to the inevitable fluctuations in your time and energy, as well as in the people and departments you oversee.

OK TO COPY

HEAVYWEIGHTS

Determining how much you should oversee

Context

When deciding how much of an organization one person can manage and lead well, remember that every situation is different. In order to determine an appropriate range of control, you must consider the person in charge, the dynamics within the department, the available resources, and extenuating factors inside and outside of the church. When the range becomes too burdensome, the church will bog down and leaders risk becoming frustrated and burned out.

Discussion

1. What do you think about the current leader's range of control in our church? Is it too broad, too narrow, or just right? Explain.
2. Is your range of control too broad, too narrow, or just right? Explain.
3. What are the dangers of a range of control that is too broad?
4. What are some characteristics of a healthy range of control?
5. What should you consider when estimating the weight of a department or a responsibility?

Activity 1

Form teams of two to four people each. Give each team twenty packets of sugar, a twelve-inch ruler, and a one-inch building block. (The building block will act as a fulcrum, but a cell phone or a large eraser may be used instead.)

Tell one team to place the ruler so that the six-inch mark is on the center of the fulcrum; tell another team to place its ruler at the five-inch mark; tell a third to place the ruler at the four-inch mark. Continue in this manner until each team has been given a different designation. Then give each team sixty seconds to stack as many sugar packets as possible while keeping its ruler in balance.

Discuss the challenges of achieving balance in this activity. Explore the importance of the placement of the fulcrum and what made each team's challenge unique. Use this activity to demonstrate how to analyze how much responsibility one person should have in overseeing portions of an organization, depending on resources, leverage, and the dynamics of each department.

Activity 2

Develop an organizational flowchart for each person represented on your staff. Help each one measure the weight of his or her various responsibilities to determine whether the range of control is healthy. If the range is too broad, discuss how you might reorganize temporarily, or for the long-term, to improve effectiveness.

OK
TO COPY

LESSON 3

LEADER TRACKS

How to spot potential leaders in your church

Identifying, recruiting, and elevating individuals with leadership skills and gifts must become a priority if we are to cope with constant changes and maximize our churches' effectiveness. Jesus did a good job of searching the throngs for a few people who had the potential to become world-class leaders.

Committed, positive, active, and outspoken people may or may not be leaders. These traits are not necessarily those that inspire groups to pursue change. Another person who may *look* like a leader but may not be one is the supertalent, the person who performs brilliantly alone but is clueless when it comes to team play and social influencing.

Here are some guidelines to help you identify leaders, regardless of their personality idiosyncrasies.

1. Who has a history of leading? Dig around just a bit, and you'll find a basketball-team captain, the president of a school club, or even the recommendation of a teacher who says, "She was a class leader. For good or for bad, people followed her." Leadership traits tend to pop up early in life.

2. Who's listening? Leaders don't always talk a lot, but when they do talk, people listen. Watch people as they interact. They are not all heard equally. Heads turn, eyes follow, and questions are aimed at people who are perceived as leaders, whether or not they are in formal positions of authority. Watch interaction in a group, and see who emerges as a leader.

3. Who's missing? People come and go from social circles, but when leaders are missing, people notice. Sad to say, the absence of most people is not significantly noticed. But when a person with leadership gifts does not show up, there is a noticeable void.

4. Who's in charge? Leaders get pretty frustrated when faced with a lack of leadership, an abandonment of service, and chaos in general. Quite often you'll hear leaders mutter to themselves or ask others, "Who's in charge?" The idea that someone should be leading is obvious to most leaders. They have an innate desire to help lead when confronted with a leadership void, whether or not they've been given an official mandate to lead.

5. Who's leading now? Over time, most leaders tend to seek out or be elevated to leadership roles. People who lead in one organization often lead in other settings and situations.

See if you can spot people with leadership gifts in various settings. Also identify those who are in roles of authority but lack leadership skills. The findings may be interesting.

LESSON 3

LEADER TRACKS

How to spot potential leaders in your church

Context

If we are going to increase leadership resources within our churches and develop people who have the ability to influence others, we must constantly be on the lookout for those who have the potential to lead.

Discussion

1. How did you come to your place of influence?

2. How do we go about recruiting leaders in our church?

3. What are our leader pools? In what areas can we detect those with leadership potential?

4. What are the challenges of finding new leaders?

5. How can we do a better job of developing those with leadership potential?

Activity 1

Ask participants to list ten people within your church who they believe have leadership potential but who are not now in a leadership role. Discuss what your current leaders can do to intentionally develop these people.

Activity 2

Before this activity, write the following descriptions on scraps of paper, one description per scrap. Prepare as many sets of instructions as you have groups of six to twelve participants. (This activity is designed for a group of six to twelve. If you have more participants, form multiple groups of six to twelve.)

1. You're the leader. Your task is to get everyone to stand up, change seats, and sit down again.
2. You're a resister. You work against the goal of the perceived leader.
3. You're an underminer. Your goal is to get people to question the perceived leader.
4. You're a questioner. You ask the perceived leader why you should participate.
5. You're a helper. You help the perceived leader get the others to follow.
6. You're a follower. Follow the person you believe to be the leader.
7. You're a follower. Follow the person you believe to be the leader.
8. You're a follower. Follow the person you believe to be the leader.
9. You're a follower. Follow the person you believe to be the leader.
10. You're a follower. Follow the person you believe to be the leader.
11. You're a follower. Follow the person you believe to be the leader.
12. You're a follower. Follow the person you believe to be the leader.

Ask participants to form groups of six to twelve, and ask each group to move to a separate area of the room and sit down. Give each person a scrap of paper with a description on it. After everyone has a description, tell participants to begin. (Adjust the number of followers according to the size of your group.)

After one or two minutes, bring everyone together to discuss these questions:

- What was your role?
- How did you know who the leader was?
- How well did your group accomplish the goal?
- How does this activity parallel real life?

L3 LEADING

Becoming a leader of leaders

Someone said, "There are two kinds of people in the world: those who say there are two kinds of people in the world and those who don't." Well, I believe there are three kinds of leaders in the world: L1, L2, and L3.

L1 leaders may not have natural leadership gifts and may not even have significant leadership potential, but they have been placed in positions of power, authority, and influence. They are in organizations that structure certain roles to wield significant influence regardless of the person holding the position (the presidency of the United States is an example of such a role). Unfortunately, when people who may be good at managing and even decision-making are expected to lead simply because their positions require them to lead, things can get frustrating. In these cases, an L1 leader can greatly improve his or her effectiveness through leadership training and significant learning. An L1 leader who doesn't understand the need for this learning will suffocate a church. We need L1 leaders. We also need to constantly train and develop them so they understand leadership.

L2 leaders are naturally gifted and have the capacity to grow and develop as leaders. Most L2 leaders seek out and are elevated to formal or informal roles of leadership. The degree of talent and gifting within this group varies. Superstar leaders tend to become household names. Great leaders are interviewed, have books written about them, and can contribute significantly to nearly any organization.

L3 leaders instinctively, and with experience and wisdom, raise and develop other leaders. L3 leaders usually are L2 leaders to some degree in that they have an innate awareness or "feel" for leadership. But often, L2 leaders never become L3 leaders because they do not know how to mentor, they do not want to share the limelight, or they feel threatened when influential people rise up around them. Many great leaders in the L2 category are good at leading an organization in the right direction but are bound by their own leadership talents. L3 leaders see their primary goal as raising up other leaders and are exponentially effective as a result. The effect of their influence eventually results in remarkable productivity that extends far beyond their individual capabilities.

In his three short years of ministry, Jesus demonstrated L3 leadership. He invested much of his time in raising up other leaders who would eventually spread the gospel message on his behalf.

What kind of leader are you?

OK TO COPY

L3 LEADING

Becoming a leader of leaders

Context

Every church needs different types of leaders, but the most overlooked type is the leader who develops leaders. Leading leaders is different from leading followers. "Role leaders" (L1) and "natural leaders" (L2) often need "leaders of leaders" (L3) to help them reach their potential, as well as to create leadership environments within their churches.

Discussion

1. What kind of a leader are you: L1, L2, or L3? Why do you think so?
2. How are leaders developed in our church?
3. What is the difference between leading followers and leading leaders?
4. What are some ways that L3 leaders can emerge in our church?
5. What is the upside of L3 leading? What is the downside?

Activity 1

Before this activity, write this statement on a piece of paper: "Leaders are naturally gifted to lead." On a second piece of paper, write, "Leaders are trained to lead."

Form two teams, and give each team one of the statements you prepared. Give teams ten minutes to prepare arguments defending their statements. Then flip a coin to see who goes first, and give each side three minutes to state its case. Afterward, ask the participants to evaluate the arguments for and against the idea that leaders are born rather than made.

Activity 2

Ask participants to form groups of three or four, then have each group write a job description for each of the three leader types: role leader (L1), natural leader (L2), and leader of leaders (L3). Ask groups to list three to five skills and expectations that might fit each type of leader. For example, role leaders might possess good people skills and a high degree of commitment to the church. Natural leaders might be good communicators, visionaries, and excellent motivators. Leaders of leaders might possess mentoring skills, experience, wisdom, and the ability to spot the potential in others.

Ask groups to consider why there are differences in the job descriptions and what kind of person would be best suited for each.

POWER UP

Sources of power and influence

Imagine that you work for a utility company and your job is to keep electricity running through the wires so that entire communities can function. To do this, you must directly or indirectly deal with a potentially lethal commodity: electrical power. Without this vital energy, people would die, and society as we know it would come to a screeching halt.

Leadership power is to a church what electrical power is to a factory or a city. You can't lead without power and influence. The term *powerless leader* is an oxymoron. Therefore, leaders must be aware of the sources from which they might obtain power. While those who seek power for its own sake are dangerous, those who avoid power may not understand its great potential for good. Leaders use power to help others accomplish what they could not achieve on their own. Here are six sources of power.

1. Personality. "Natural" leaders have the ability to attract attention and convince people to follow them. This power is based on physical, psychological, and relational characteristics.

2. Position. Power may stem from a position that is endowed with influence within an organization. In this case the seat holder becomes a power wielder.

3. Expertise. The ability to perform an important skill or task can in itself be a source of influence and power.

4. References. Knowing influential or powerful people can also be a source of power.

5. Information. Possessing specific or vital information enables people to control situations and wield influence.

6. Reward. The ability to reward others is a source of power.

Most true leadership influence stems from these six sources. Leaders tap into these sources in different ways and at different times. Scripture says that God-followers were not given a Spirit of timidity, but of power, self-discipline, and love (2 Timothy 1:7). The world and your church need more people who pursue power for the right reasons and are catalysts of positive change.

LESSON 5

POWER UP

Sources of power and influence

Context

Power may be controversial. If you seek power improperly or for the wrong reasons, you may be perceived as a power-monger and a detriment to your church. If you are unaware of the need for power, or if you do not understand the sources of power, then you will be less able to serve others well. Effective leaders realize both the sources of power and its importance.

Discussion

1. What are the inherent dangers of power?
2. What are the positive attributes of power?
3. Have you known people in leadership roles who lacked adequate power? What was the result?
4. Think of leaders you know. Which of the six sources of power do they rely upon?
5. Think of someone you've known whose power from one or more of these sources has diminished. Why did this person lose influence, and what was the result within the church?

Activity 1

Before this activity, list the following power sources on a white board or sheet of newsprint. Give participants a sheet of paper and instruct them to copy the list on the paper. Ask them to determine how much of their power stems from each source and to indicate the percentage next to each one. (The total should equal one hundred.) Ask each participant which one he or she would

like to cultivate in order to lead more effectively.

- personality _____
- position _____
- expertise _____
- references _____
- information _____
- reward _____

Activity 2

Before this activity, place varying amounts of Monopoly money in envelopes so that you have one envelope per participant.

Ask participants each to list two to four things they would like to obtain for their areas of responsibility (such as a new computer, a budget for advertising, and extra staff). Ask participants to compile their lists, deleting similar or duplicate requests. (For example, if two people want a new computer, the group would list "new computer" only once.) Randomly distribute the envelopes you prepared earlier. Then auction off the items on the wish list, one by one, awarding each to the highest bidder.

Afterward, ask participants, "How was this activity like and unlike situations you face in leadership every day? What are appropriate uses of power? What are inappropriate uses?"

19

THE SELLING SOILS

LESSON 6

The role of selling in leadership

Everyone is in sales. If you are not selling cars, clothes, or widgets, you are selling services, ideas, and best of all...yourself. All sales people are not leaders, but all leaders must sell. Leaders are vendors of new ideas, purveyors of hope. They often sell the intangible, the stuff of dreams and visions. Many frustrated leaders fail to recognize that their proposed changes will be met by different reactions, based upon the varying degrees of receptivity among their followers.

Jesus' parable in Matthew 13:3-8 is instructive here: A seed fell on a path where it was eaten by a bird. Another seed fell on rock, sprouted, then died because it couldn't develop roots in the shallow soil. A third seed fell on soil but was choked by neighboring weeds. A fourth seed fell on fertile soil and produced an abundance. Jesus used this parable in the context of another message, but his metaphor also illustrates my point about receptivity.

The seed eaten by the bird represents situations in which the recipient is completely closed to the message. Don't invest a lot of time breaking down a closed door. You'll only lower your self-esteem and frustrate the other party. Although you may eventually convince this person, you are apt to waste a lot of time and energy when you could be seeking more fertile ground. Cut your losses and go on. Realize that you cannot convince everyone. A new idea or vision is not likely to find a home here.

The seed that sprouted then withered represents the person who at first is keen on your offer but has no compelling reason to "buy." Quick sells often do more harm than good. Make sure your potential buyer understands your idea (or service or product). Take time to cultivate the soil, demonstrating how and why the product will benefit the buyer, so that when the seed is planted and sprouts, it has a chance of bearing fruit. Pre-sale preparation is vital for post-sale fulfillment. Sometimes people nod their heads but never consider the ramifications of their assent. Education, scriptural teaching, and relationship building are essential if this person is to remain committed.

The seed that sprouts but is choked by weeds represents someone who initially wants to buy but is then sidetracked by other claims on his or her attention or resources. People are bombarded by so many messages competing for their limited time, money, and attention that your message may easily be crowded out. Recognize that the first part of the sale is very delicate and must be treated with care and loving attention, then take time to follow up. Do not confuse preoccupation with disinterest. Nurture the young sprout until it grows

 **LESSON 6** THE SELLING SOILS

strong by investing time in the relationship. Communicate frequently, foster accountability. and allow the roots to take hold.

The seed that bore fruit is the slam-dunk deal that was just waiting for you. Sometimes it's just a matter of timing; at other times it's the result of intentional preparation. We all dream of these scenarios, but they are a minority. Keep trying. Don't give up. Sometimes finding the right selling soil is merely a numbers game. Don't stop until you find it. Develop a mind-set that allows you to recognize this fertile soil.

Here's to a bumper crop!

THE SELLING SOILS

The role of selling in leadership

Context

Leaders must sell their ideas and goals to potential supporters, staff, funders, bosses, peers, and sometimes even friends and family members. A leader's ability to do this is directly related to how well he or she understands the audience, the various soils onto which the seed is sown.

Discussion

1. Why is it important to evaluate people's readiness to hear a plan, goal, or vision before you begin talking to them about it?
2. Can you think of a time you had a good idea but the time was not right for it? What happened?
3. What are some ways of turning barren soil into fertile soil, preparing people to accept an idea?
4. One of the most common failures in sales is not asking for the sale. How do you ask people for their commitment, without leaving them or the idea hanging?
5. Many leaders tend to blame people for not responding to them favorably, instead of considering their responsibility to evaluate people's receptivity, prepare the soil, and then sell well. Why do you think this is so?

Activity 1

To prepare for this activity, write the following words, each on its own slip of paper: *leaders, cold, cool, warm,* and *hot*. Place the five slips of paper in a bowl. Think of a single idea, goal, or plan pertaining to your church, such as a marketing campaign or a new facility. (The idea may be factual or fictional.)

Form five groups of one or more people each. Ask one person from each group to take a slip of paper from the bowl. Tell groups what their roles will be in the role-play: The members of the leader group should try to sell the idea to the entire group. The members of the cold group should respond by stating reasons the idea won't work. The members of the cool group should respond less negatively than those of the cold group but offer few positive responses. The members of the warm group should respond positively but be a bit reserved toward the idea. The members of the hot group should respond enthusiastically, providing even more ideas to support the plan.

This is a fun process that will help your staff understand the importance of evaluating receptivity before pursuing an idea.

Activity 2

Gather a plain rock, a rock that is partially covered with dirt, a weed, and fertile potting soil. Place each item on a table. (You may use photographs of the items instead.)

Tell participants that the plain rock represents a negative reaction; the rock with dirt on it represents rejection because those hearing the idea aren't ready for it; the weed represents an initially positive response that dies due to competing interests for time, money, and resources; and the fertile potting soil represents an enthusiastic, positive response. Ask participants to brainstorm about organizational goals and new ideas and write each idea on its own self-stick note. After the brainstorming session, ask your team to place each note beside the item that represents the likely reaction of your church to the idea. Together, determine which ideas should be shelved while readiness is increased. Then decide how to enhance receptivity and override competing interests in order to pursue the church's most important goals.

SHARPENING THE AX

The importance of personal growth

Have you ever tried chopping wood with a dull ax? It's not a pretty sight. Trying to lead effectively with dull thinking is just as frustrating, and after weeks in the trenches it's easy to become stale. We usually don't recognize staleness setting in, but our lack of creativity and new ideas ultimately results in dated practices and ineffectiveness.

God tells us that he's doing something new, that he's not satisfied with merely perpetuating the status quo: "Forget the former things; do not dwell on the past. See, I am doing a new thing! Now it springs up; do you not perceive it?" (Isaiah 43:18-19a).

The "new thing" touted by a popular Mexican restaurant is the freshness of its food. The motto is "nothing canned," and the goal is to prepare everything fresh. That's an appropriate leadership goal as well, as canned ideas and programs rarely fit unique and changing churches. Fresh leadership requires that we get up a little earlier and do a lot of our own kitchen work.

Attending a professional-growth conference may require a significant investment of time, money, and energy. The tyranny of the urgent tempts us to chop a little longer with the dull ax, but among top achievers and those who want to be, sharpening the ax is essential. Top-quality learning experiences are always worth the investment. But don't expect a mother lode; a few golden nuggets of information or wisdom will make the experience worthwhile.

Sometimes the greatest benefits are not the ideas gleaned directly from the conference (or book, seminar, video, or audiocassette), but the thoughts that come to you within that context. Be sure to keep a pen and paper, laptop, or Palm Pilot within reach for recording your hybrid ideas. They are the best ones, and you'll want to flesh them out in your own life and church. Remember that they probably wouldn't have occurred to you if you had remained on the job, dealing with the day-to-day, practical issues at hand. Leaders have to be proactive to be effective. Periodic leaves of absence to investigate new thoughts and practices are every bit as much a part of leading as staying in the office to fight fires.

What have you done lately to sharpen your ax and stay fresh? What is the last book you read, and what did you gain from it? (Articulating what you gained is a sign that you really did get something out of it.) What was the last seminar or conference you attended? What ideas from the experience have you implemented? What are your successful associates and peers reading? With whom are they networking? Where are they going for new ideas? Go to the grindstone, sharpen that ax, then chop, chop, chop.

LESSON 7

SHARPENING THE AX

The importance of personal growth

Context

While we run the real risk of becoming idea junkies in this information age, we run a greater risk of becoming dull and set in our ways. Busyness often perpetuates the notion that we have no time to sharpen the ax because there are "too many trees to cut." Regular, periodic thought stimulators can get us out of mental and emotional ruts. Continually evaluate new ideas for keeping your staff and organization growing.

Discussion

1. Name a book you've read recently, a tape you've listened to, or a workshop you've attended. How did it help you?
2. What are ways to assess the potential of a conference in order to justify the investment?
3. How might we, as a leadership team, share with one another the ideas we've gleaned through our individual reading and conference attendance?
4. How do you encourage the people on your team to remain sharp?
5. Think of an example in our church of the status quo being maintained by a dull ax. What can we do to improve?

Activity 1

Before the activity, gather four oranges, two dull butter knives, and two sharp steak knives.

Give an orange and a knife to each of four participants, and give participants fifteen seconds to cut their oranges into wedges for the rest of the staff to eat. Discuss the results, then compare this activity to the need to continually sharpen leadership skills.

Activity 2

Form groups of three to five people. Provide each group with two sheets of poster board and two markers. Ask each group to draw a simple picture, symbol, or graphic on both sheets. (The graphic may represent an idea, or it can be meaningless.) Give each group one pair of scissors, and tell participants to use the scissors to cut out the picture on one sheet of poster board. Then tell them to use their hands to tear the drawing from the second sheet of poster board. Tell them that everyone must participate in both the cutting and tearing. Compare the results, discussing the pros and cons of each process. Finally, compare this activity to the challenges and benefits of staying sharp as leaders.

NEW PATCHES

Leaders as innovators

Change is constant. The primary responsibility of leaders is to initiate necessary change and to respond to change. Leadership would be unnecessary in an unchanging environment; management and administration would do. The leadership scarcity that people have bemoaned during the last decade has more to do with the number of changes society produced than it does the number of leaders. Chances are the perception that we are turning out fewer leaders than ever is not accurate. On the other hand, the amount and degree of change has definitely accelerated. As changes increase, the real and perceived need for leaders intensifies; thus the demand for leadership books, seminars, academic programs, and other resources has also risen.

All leaders are not innovators, just as all innovators are not leaders. In fact, only a small percentage of people are truly innovative. But all leaders respond to change and encourage innovation in others. Innovators have the innate and cultivated ability to digest thoughts, concepts, and experiences and, from them, create other ideas. A larger number of people possess latent or developed leadership skills. To lead is to catalyze others to adopt a vision, a new direction, and necessary change.

Jesus told us not to sew an unshrunk patch of fabric onto well-worn material because, after it's washed, the patch will tear away from the garment, making the hole worse than it was originally (Matthew 9:16). In the same way, leaders should be sure innovations will fit their churches. Most people resist change because they are creatures of habit and prefer to remain in their comfort zones. This resistance is what can make promoting innovation and initiating change such an uphill battle. But pursuing innovations that will improve your church is your responsibility as a leader.

Now more than ever, the need for more and better leaders exists. We need leaders who are willing to push the envelope, continually respond to change, and proactively seek innovation. The future is a scary place for most people, but leaders shine a beam of light to brighten the path and create hope.

Think about how you can catalyze positive change. Jot down ten changes that would make your church more productive and responsive.

LESSON 8

NEW PATCHES

Leaders as innovators

Context

Keeping new ideas flowing into a church is vital in times of constant change. Being averse to innovation makes churches or ministries poor stewards; perpetuating their past may jeopardize their future.

While not all ideas and innovations are worthy of pursuit, the process of introducing new ideas is essential. *How* new ideas are introduced is often more important than *what* new ideas are introduced.

Discussion

1. What is one new idea that our church has recently pursued?
2. What was the origin of the idea?
3. What were the challenges of discovering, shaping, and implementing the innovation?
4. What are some factors that might be preventing you from pursuing new ideas in your area of responsibility? What can you do about them?
5. Discuss the way new ideas are introduced; how they are approved, rejected, or shaped; and how they are implemented in our church.

Activity 1

Before this activity, write a memo describing an idea that is nonsensical, silly, or far-fetched. (For example, you could say that new office hours will be from 6 a.m. to 8 a.m., Tuesday through Saturday. Or you could say that all offices will be eliminated in order to save money and that the staff will be working in a single, large room, where each person will have a laptop and table space.) State in the memo that the change will be implemented in two weeks. Distribute the memo to participants, and ask them to spend five minutes deciding how to adopt the change. At the end of this process, discuss similarities between responses to your outrageous change and feedback on almost any new idea, good or bad, that is introduced to a church.

Activity 2

Ask each person to write down one new idea he or she would like to see implemented in the coming year. Ask each participant to include notes that address the following questions:

- Who is the idea's champion, the person who will shepherd the innovation?
- How ready are others to receive the idea? Rate their receptivity on a scale from one to five, with one being opposed and five being very receptive.
- How should the idea be modified to make it more effective?
- What resources (time, space, staffing, and so on) will the idea require?
- What might have to end or be reduced if this new idea is implemented?
- What are the benefits of implementing the new idea and the risks of not implementing it?
- What are we missing?

Finally, have each person pitch his or her idea to one other staff member in the meeting and get a response that includes initial concerns, potential objections, and unanswered questions.

LEADERSHIP POKER

Determining the point of diminishing returns

In many ways, leaders are gamblers. They wager on unknown outcomes. In the church, we may refer to this as operating in the faith dimension. But leaders have to be adept at recognizing points of diminishing returns and constantly assessing the ratio of input to output to ensure they invest their time and energies where they will count most.

Jesus talked about a pearl dealer who found a pearl of great worth, sold all he had, and bought it (Matthew 13:45-46). Sometimes we fail to recognize pearls of great value and settle for less; at other times we pay too much for faux pearls. Leaders must be able to recognize when a situation deserves continued investment and when it is time to end that investment. Just as we are told to invest in worthy pearls, we're also warned about casting pearls before swine (Matthew 7:6). The latter represents poor stewardship of resources.

Every proposed significant task or activity should be scrutinized to estimate what it will produce and what it will cost. For example, every church should strive for excellence, but a leader must recognize the point at which excellence becomes perfectionism and the costs begin to outweigh the benefits. It may be worthwhile to improve quality from 80 percent to 90 percent. But reaching 95 percent may cost 10 to 30 percent more. Leaders are constantly asking, "Is the extra effort worth it?" Many of these decisions are subjective and intuitive, which is why leadership is more of an art than a science.

In the same way that a leader evaluates the cost-to-benefit ratio of organizational programs and tasks, he or she must also evaluate his or her own activities to determine whether the results justify the time and effort.

Recognizing the point of diminishing returns is a hallmark of good leadership. Is a sole, stubborn parishioner worth further investment of your time if that investment causes you to pass up potential newcomers? Is one team member consuming more than his or her share of your attention so that the entire team suffers? Which of your daily activities is keeping you from doing something that might yield a higher dividend for your church? Is your investment in a certain person going to create the most influence possible? Are you doing tasks or developing task-doers? There's a big difference.

Wise leaders recognize the points of diminishing return. Strong leaders are able to make the often difficult decision to cut their losses for the sake of greater productivity. While it may seem foolish to cut branches that are bearing fruit, enabling the vines to produce even more fruit requires that kind of pruning.

LESSON 9

LEADERSHIP POKER

Determining the point of diminishing returns

Context

All ideas are not created equal. Some produce more and better outcomes than others. Leaders must constantly assess the input-to-output ratio, reducing resource-wasting activities and increasing productive ones. The temptation is to prolong the life of good ideas, often without recognizing when they have ceased to be effective. The key is to estimate when increasing input will bring maximum output and when it will simply cost you or your church unnecessary resources.

Discussion

1. Think of one thing you are doing now that seems to require more effort than it is worth. What will you save by ending the practice? What will you lose?
2. What is an example of an idea or program that you invested in that produced diminishing returns?
3. Nearly all ideas have shelf lives, which means that something that worked yesterday might not be as productive today. How do you know when an idea has run its course?
4. Were you ever pleasantly surprised by something that produced significant results with very little investment?
5. Can you think of an idea that seemed promising but, in spite of major investments, didn't work? What did you learn?

Activity 1

Form groups of three to five. Tell participants that they are to pretend that they are all marooned on a deserted island with a single raft. They have the following supplies but can take only half of them on the three-day voyage to the shipping channel. Give groups ten minutes to determine what to leave, what to take, and why.

- Meal packs
- Flare gun
- Shark repellent
- Fresh water
- First-aid kit
- Radio transmitter
- Battery for transmitter
- Paddles
- Nautical map
- Heart medicine for one member with a health problem

Have each group share its list with the others and offer its rationale. If time permits, discuss whether the processes that groups used to determine their lists were adequate.

Activity 2

Ask participants to each list ten activities they do within the scope of their normal responsibilities. Then ask them to rank each activity in order of importance (with one being most important and ten being least). Tell them to assign a required output value to each (with one representing low output, two representing medium output, and three representing high output). Ask participants to discuss what this activity has revealed about outcomes, priorities, and appropriate investment of resources.

BLIND SPOTS

Understanding the difference between perception and reality

Leaders are not immune to blind spots. Studies reveal that a significant percentage of workers believe managers are not as qualified as the managers consider themselves to be. Are team members just more critical, or are leaders' perceptions unrealistic?

Here are five suggestions for eliminating blind spots.

1. Assume there is a blind spot, regardless of size. This will help you consistently consider what you might do to identify and reduce it. There is always room for improvement.

2. Request feedback. Many leaders assume that one-way communication is sufficient, but the leader who wants to know when he or she misses the mark needs multiple feedback loops. You can choose from a growing number of 360-degree evaluation methods to see your behavior from the perspectives of those who work with you.

3. Reward negative feedback. Silence may be golden, but it's also corrosive to quality leadership. Often requests for feedback are greeted with silence because people don't want to be punished for negative responses. Motivated team players feel threatened around defensive leaders. Teach and model how to give negative feedback constructively, and welcome it as your friend.

4. Solicit feedback from third parties. Most feedback gleaned directly from those who report to you will be guarded and edited. If you want honest-to-goodness perceptions, ask neutral third parties to gather the feedback, perform exit interviews, and periodically experience your church or ministry to help you see what others inside do not see or are unwilling to relate to you.

5. Develop trustworthy grapevines. Some leaders remain in their offices, in self-imposed exile. A lot of leaders surround themselves with fans who are either oblivious to the leader's blind spots or willing to overlook them based on friendships. To counteract these tendencies, get out and mingle with the folks you work with and those who work with them. Hang out with your staff. Get off the platform, and greet people in the sanctuary. Aloofness guarantees larger blind spots. Make sure your grapevine consists of varied and reliable sources. Taking the pulse of your church may be informal and spontaneous, but it must also be intentional and ongoing.

Our first temptation is to deny that we have blind spots. Jesus revealed the spiritual blind spots of the religious leaders of his day, and he was eventually crucified for it. Revealing blind spots can be dangerous. But secure, honest leaders welcome such information, knowing that blind spots only diminish their effectiveness.

LESSON 10

BLIND SPOTS

Understanding the difference between perception and reality

Context

Someone once said that none of us is as good as we think we are or as bad as our enemies think we are. None of us has a perfect perspective on our leadership. Our perspectives are always incomplete. Honest feedback will always give us crucial opportunities to grow and improve.

Discussion

1. Can you think of a negative experience that resulted from one of your blind spots? Tell what happened.
2. Why is it impossible to avoid all blind spots?
3. What are your blind spots in the areas for which you are responsible? How can you reduce them?
4. Who do you trust to provide reliable feedback, even if it is not positive? What kind of person do you not trust?
5. What processes to uncover blind spots can you develop in your area of responsibility?

Activity 1

Arrange the chairs in a circle, then place one chair in the center of the circle. Distribute paper and pencils, and ask the participants to pretend that they are in an art class. Ask a "model" to sit in the middle of the circle, then ask the others to draw what they see. After five minutes, ask participants to hold up their sketches. Discuss how this activity relates to the ways churches analyze people, programs, and events. Solicit ideas for obtaining more holistic perspectives.

Activity 2

Before the activity, cut a picture from a magazine, or write a message on a sheet of paper. Cut the picture or paper into six to twelve pieces, depending on the number of participants, and place each piece in its own envelope. Randomly number the envelopes, beginning with number one and working up.

Give an envelope to each participant. In numerical order and one at a time, ask each participant to open the envelope and place the piece on a table. Before a new envelope is opened, ask the group to guess what the finished picture or message is. After each guess, ask for the next envelope to be opened. After all the components have been correctly pieced together, discuss these questions:

- If each piece represents one person's perspective, why is it important to gather multiple perspectives?
- Were there certain pieces that proved to be more helpful than others in determining the final view? How does this relate to leadership situations?
- What would have happened if you had based your decision solely on early guesses?

MURDERER OR GOD?

How success and failure affect how people perceive leaders

After being shipwrecked, the Apostle Paul and the ship's crew found themselves on the island of Malta. The islanders made a fire to provide warmth for the stranded voyagers, and Paul gathered brushwood for the fire. As he added more wood, a snake emerged from it and latched onto his hand. The islanders saw this and said to each other, "This man must be a murderer; for though he escaped from the sea, Justice has not allowed him to live." But Paul shook the viper into the fire and suffered no ill effects from the bite. The islanders then thought Paul must be a god because he survived a deadly snakebite (Acts 28:1-6).

This story illustrates the fine line that separates perceptions of us as good or evil. Perceptions of leaders are largely determined by the degree of success they achieve. When a church is expanding and growth is good, the pastor is often considered a wonder. When attendance falls and malaise characterizes the congregation, the same leader may be considered utterly incompetent.

The tendency to give either too much or too little credit to leaders is quite common. Leaders of failing churches are usually not as bad as they seem, just as leaders of successful ones are usually not as good as they appear. This is not to suggest that good leaders really are not good and that incompetent leaders are not truly incompetent. The point is that this positive and negative exaggeration is a reality of leadership. Whether perceptions are true or false, they are nonetheless important because people act on them. Leaders are only as influential as their followers and teammates allow them to be.

To be effective, leaders must be aware of vacillating perceptions among those they are called to lead. Leaders should never be overconfident when things are going well, for just as quickly as they are hailed as heroes, they can be condemned. Simply knowing this should help leaders remain humble amid the applause and be encouraged when they are criticized.

A healthy, balanced leader will temper both compliments and complaints. By riding the popularity-poll roller coaster, we weaken our ability to lead. Leaders are best when they rely on character and consistency over the long haul rather than emotions that can change with every new set of circumstances. Leaders cannot ignore the opinions of others, but they will never be strong if they rely too heavily upon them. Too much applause can make us susceptible to a prideful fall. With too little affirmation, we're prone to discouragement, losing sight of the potential that lies below the surface of every situation.

LESSON

MURDERER OR GOD?

How success and failure affect how people perceive leaders

Context

People are fickle. They can be swayed easily by gossip, innuendo, subjective perceptions, and circumstantial evidence. To be effective, leaders must understand this reality and learn to rely on God, rather than people, for a true understanding of their worth.

Discussion

1. Can you think of an example of circumstances creating the perception that you were worse than you really were?
2. Can you think of a time when circumstances created the perception that you were more talented or successful than you really were?
3. Generally, when can you rely on circumstances to gauge your success?
4. Why do you think people are so quick to base their opinions of leaders on limited evidence?
5. What can leaders do to avoid being adversely affected by the opinions of others?

Activity 1

Deal three playing cards to everyone. Instruct participants to add up the face value of their cards (face cards are worth ten points each; all others are worth five) and state their totals. Tell the group that, for the purpose of this activity, the most successful people are the ones with the highest totals. Reward each person with individual pieces of candy, giving more candy to those with higher totals. Discuss whether this reward is fair; then lead the group into a discussion of how the human desire for fairness factors into their emotional responses as leaders.

Activity 2

Form teams of three or four. Give each team ten dominoes, placing them facedown on the table as you distribute them. Begin the game by placing a domino faceup in the center of the table. Then have teams take turns turning over one domino each. When a domino matches the end of the original one, instruct players to place that tile in the middle, connecting dots. Then give the next team a turn. If the dots do not match, tell the same team to continue to turn over tiles until it can play a domino. The first team to play all tiles wins. If none of the teams can finish, the team with the fewest remaining tiles wins.

Discuss how much of this game was determined by luck and how much was determined by skill. Discuss the various factors that contribute to success, such as luck, timing, talent, God, perseverance, and competition.

VERBAL LEADING

How words affect influence

The Bible tells us that "the tongue also is a fire, a world of evil among the parts of the body. It corrupts the whole person, sets the whole course of his life on fire, and is itself set on fire by hell" (James 3:6). Conversely, speech has more power to nurture love and hope than any other tool available to humanity. Many of us grossly underestimate the power of our words and the importance of crafting what we say and how we say it. This is especially true for leaders because of the magnifying glass effect.

Things placed under a magnifying glass appear larger than they really are. In the same way, the words of leaders assume more importance than they really possess. When a leader communicates fear or criticism, or even makes a mildly satirical comment, the reverberation can be significant. One casual, offhand comment uttered by a pastor can devastate leaders, peers, and congregants. Most of us have scratched our heads in wonderment that a casual comment could be so exaggerated by a listener.

The words of nonleaders are not as significant; those who aren't in a position of leadership are freer to express opinions, forecasts, and irritations. Leaders are wise when they bite their tongues and temper their views. Leaders are only human, but they must always remember that they are also social and organizational architects. Their responsibility is not simply to themselves, but also to those whom they serve. Leaders who frequently claim their right to free speech usually end up exercising their right to bear arms and shoot themselves in the foot.

On the other hand, leaders can make a significant difference by uttering words of faith, hope, and love. When they use their mouths to communicate a positive vision, to offer words of encouragement and affirmation, and to convey esteem, the entire church benefits. When a leader smiles, gives a thumbs up, writes a note of thanks, or looks a team member in the eye while saying, "Good job!" the effect lingers long after he or she has walked away, and others will emulate this kind of behavior.

According to the Bible, the key to governing the tongue is cultivating character. The mouth is the window to the soul. What comes out someone's mouth is an indicator of what's inside. Good wells give good water; foul wells deliver nasty water. Leaders must remind themselves that their leading is not about themselves but about others, and they must constantly monitor their speech. Far too often, leaders allow their own anxiety and stress to infect their speech, and meetings become therapy sessions in which they unload their frustrations—only to burden and debilitate their teams.

LESSON 12

VERBAL LEADING

How words affect influence

Context

An essential leadership tool is the ability to communicate orally. Because a leader is in a position of influence, a leader's words are magnified to the point that they have greater potential to bring about good or bad outcomes. This magnification means that leaders, more than others, must guard their emotions, select their words carefully, and intentionally communicate those things that will positively influence their churches.

Discussion

1. Describe a time someone's words hurt you.
2. Have you ever been surprised by the impact of your words on someone you influence? Describe the experience.
3. Can you think of a time you were inspired by a leader's words?
4. What comes to mind when you think about improving what you say?
5. How can we help others to be more accountable for their words so that they leave positive impressions wherever they go?

Activity 1

Before this activity, gather four disposable cups with lids. Pour a few tablespoons of ammonia in one cup, rose petals in another, minced garlic in another, and a few teaspoons of vanilla in the fourth.

Blindfold four participants, and ask each to identify the contents of one of the cups by sniffing it.

Discuss how each person, without seeing the cup's contents, could tell whether the contents smelled good or bad. Relate this experience to oral communication, making the point that, when we speak, we leave a good or bad aroma. People are often more affected by how our words "smell" than by their actual content.

Activity 2

Before this activity, find a picture of a villain and a picture of a hero.

Give a pad of self-stick notes to each participant, and ask everyone to think of positive and negative words or phrases that are common in organizations and team environments. Ask participants to write these words or phrases, one per note. As participants are writing, tape the two pictures to a wall. Gather the notepads.

Refer to the old Western melodramas in which the audience booed the villain and cheered the hero. Lead participants in practicing boos and cheers. Then tell them that, after you read each word or phrase, they will respond by booing or cheering, depending upon their reaction to it. Based on their response, place each self-stick note under the appropriate picture. Finally, burn or tear up the negative words to symbolize your leaders' commitment to avoid them.

LESSON

THE PRINCIPAL'S LIST

Setting your standards

Our fifth-grade son once invited us to an awards assembly at his school. The purpose of the assembly was to honor the fifth-graders who had made the principal's list and the honor roll. I was intrigued by the discrepancy in the number of award recipients from various classes. One class had only three award recipients while another had no less than twenty. While one teacher was obviously too hard on the kids, the other was too lenient.

What is a good standard for achievement? Leaders must constantly assess whether their teams' goals are too hard or too easy and the ramifications of those standards. Here are the advantages and disadvantages of difficult and lenient standards.

Advantages of lenient standards

• Self-esteem is raised, and love is communicated.

• The leader is often well-liked.

• Team building and affirmation occur.

• Good grades are more fun to give than bad ones.

Disadvantages of lenient standards

• Overall standards are lowered.

• Individuals who really excel are discouraged.

• People aren't adequately prepared for the real world.

• Long-term respect and team strength are compromised.

Advantages of difficult standards

• Higher standards of quality are set.

• Higher achievers are motivated to accomplish more.

• The leader is respected.

• The leader saves personal energy and sometimes resources.

Disadvantages of difficult standards

• Low-performing individuals may become discouraged.

• A team that's given high standards may be disheartened if other teams are given lower standards.

• A leader might not be well-liked.

• Individuals may give up because they feel the standards are impossible to meet.

There is no perfect standard for rewarding team members. Each situation is different, but generally I believe that most leaders would do well to reward more than they do. God is very gracious, but he also maintains high standards of excellence. Perhaps we need his wisdom in setting standards in our own churches.

LESSON 13

THE PRINCIPAL'S LIST

Setting your standards

Context

Establishing standards of quality and performance is a significant challenge for leaders for several reasons. First, leaders tend to have higher energy levels than other people do, and their motivations are different; they shouldn't require the same level of energy and the same motivations in the people they lead. Second, leaders must understand that different people are motivated by different things. Individuals might be motivated primarily by a sense of fulfillment, by money, by pride, by recognition, by a sense of responsibility to their community, by their faith, or by a combination of these and other factors. Finally, leaders should understand that people attach varying values to different methods of recognition. Some prefer privately spoken words of affirmation, some prefer material rewards, and some prefer the applause of their peers.

Discussion

1. What is the best way to establish standards?
2. Can you think of an example in which expectations were too high? too low? What was the result?
3. Are our standards too lenient or too demanding?
4. What can we do to establish more reasonable standards?
5. What kinds of rewards can we provide?

Activity 1

Form three teams of one to four people each. Give one team a jigsaw puzzle intended for preschoolers, give the second team a jigsaw puzzle intended for first- to third-graders, and give the third team a jigsaw puzzle intended for adults. Tell participants that each team that completes its puzzle within the allotted time will receive a prize. Give teams one to three minutes to fit together their pieces. When time is up, give members of the winning team a small reward, such as a piece of candy or a gift certificate for a cup of coffee. Then discuss the effects of this kind of inequity in tasks and rewards. Relate the activity to your own church, and lead the group in brainstorming ways to equalize standards and determine appropriate rewards.

Finally, give members of the other teams the same reward you gave to members of the "winning" team.

Activity 2

Form two teams, and announce that everyone will compete in a spelling bee. One person from one team will be asked to stand and spell a given word. If the word is spelled correctly, that team will be awarded one point. Then a member of the other team will be asked to stand and spell a different word. The bee will continue until everyone has spelled one word, and the team with the most points will win.

Give the following words, adding more if necessary:

Team 1	Team 2
hypochondriac	*game*
archaeology	*can*
regurgitation	*hope*

Team 1 is likely to lose because it was given more difficult words. Encourage participants to relate this activity to the standards in your church by asking questions such as, Why was the competition unfair? How are life and ministry unfair at times? and What can you do as a leader to level the playing field in your ministry? Brainstorm ways to eliminate inequities and ways to provide meaningful, motivational rewards.

STAFF ROLES

Four primary organizational roles

There is a place for everyone involved in any organized endeavor. Sometimes leaders can help themselves by categorizing the people in their organizations to determine how their gifts might best be used. Here are four categories that might help: natural leaders, influencers, collaborators, and nonparticipants. Understanding these categories will allow you to establish more realistic expectations. It will also allow you to help the people in your church reach their potential.

Natural Leaders—These people are naturally gifted with the ability to understand people, define and achieve goals, and influence others. These qualities tend to reveal themselves in childhood and adolescence. Certainly not everyone can be a leader. Most people are not wired for leadership and have no inclination to lead.

Influencers—Some people have the natural ability to influence others. A naturally influential person may not be particularly influential in a church because he or she lacks experience or interest in it. Those who are actively influential in a church may have become influential through relationships, tenure, expertise, or sheer work and commitment. They may or may not be in an official leadership capacity. Though influential, many do not posses leadership gifts. Influencers are often overlooked, but they are important to the success of any church. They can multiply a leader's influence, just as an amplifier increases a stereo speaker's output. On the other hand, they can thwart, change, and bog down leadership. Although influencers will never be outstanding individual leaders, they should be trained to their potential.

Collaborators—These people are basically followers, but they are not necessarily passive. If a collaborator is involved in leadership, he or she provides at least a mild collaborative influence. These team members may or may not support the leader or the vision. Collaborators may be influential in their ability to fulfill a dream, to buck a vision, or to support or deny certain leaders. While active collaborators should not be confused with leaders, twenty-first century leadership recognizes these participants as vital members of the leadership process.

Nonparticipants—Certain people may be physically present, but emotionally absent, in your church. These people are essentially spectators. Nonparticipants may become collaborators, influencers, or leaders, but at this point in time, they are uninvolved. Leaders need to consider their numbers and potential without fooling themselves into thinking these nonparticipants are participants. Even great leaders can't get everyone to buy into their dreams.

LESSON 14

STAFF ROLES

Four primary organizational roles

Context

To understand the impact different people have on organizations, it is helpful to determine if they are natural leaders, influencers, collaborators, or nonparticipants. Categorizing people in this way can help leaders establish realistic expectations of their staffs while developing them to their full potential. For example, a committed collaborator should not be promoted to a position of leadership merely because he or she is active. Another example is that someone in a position of leadership cannot be assumed to be a natural leader; even so, it's important to recognize that the person has influence by virtue of his or her position.

Discussion

1. Think of people in your church who are nonparticipants, spectators who aren't emotionally involved in the church. What should your attitude be toward them?
2. Think of individuals who are collaborators, team members who participate but have little influence. What should your attitude be toward them?
3. List people who, through relationships, position, tenure, or skills, are influencers but aren't natural leaders. How can you develop these people more effectively?
4. Name people who are leaders because of their natural gifts and have proven themselves as such.
5. What are the benefits of identifying which categories the individuals in your church fall into? What are the risks?

Activity 1

Before the activity, prepare to play a game of Categories. Think of four categories, then list ten items within each category. For example, if the category is pets, you might list dog, cat, goldfish, parakeet, hamster, horse, guinea pig, lizard, gerbil, and turtle.

Form two teams. Give one team a category and thirty seconds to call out items within that category while a scorer listens and checks items off the list. Then give the other team a category and ten seconds to call out items. After both teams have played twice, discuss the idea that items in a category can be different without being inherently good or bad. Discuss the risk of lumping people in your church together so that you fail to distinguish between leaders, influencers, and followers.

Activity 2

The game of chess can illustrate the complex nature of leadership. Set up a chess board, and explain the power and moving ability of each piece. (If you don't know how to play, ask someone who does to explain the game.) Explain that all the pieces on each side are working together toward a common goal. Then focus attention on the strategic roles of the rook, knight, and bishop. These pieces illustrate the influencers in a church. They are not pawns (collaborators) or natural leaders (the king and queen), but they can make or break the game. List some people in your church who seem to fit these four categories, and brainstorm ways to develop and better utilize these people. (Be sensitive to labeling; don't run the risk of offending others by the use of terms such as "pawn," "king," and "queen.")

LEADER REST

The importance of rest and renewal

Most leaders are wired to be self-motivated, high-energy people. Leaders who are not motivated are either undergoing times of transition or are burned out. Once while attending the Phoenix Open PGA tournament, I tried to figure out why so many executive types enjoy the game. The time-to-adrenaline ratio seems all wrong to me. Then I looked around at the beautiful greens and the mountain vistas and thought about golf's quiet protocol. I realized then why busy execs enjoy these hours of escape from pressing schedules; a golf course is a place to unwind.

We all need to unwind in order to stay wound. Jesus often retreated after a pressing day to spend time alone and in prayer, seemingly aloof to the endless needs and opportunities around him. People who are in the business of making important decisions that affect others need a healthy, balanced perspective. Times away to contemplate, pray, and regain this perspective are vital to staying the course.

Organizational growth, staff transitions, changes in the community, facility limitations, finances, and the day-to-day pressures of leadership naturally create stress, but leaders are often unaware that their anxiety levels are rising. Inevitably, though, stress rises to the surface in the form of frayed emotions, low batteries, and a desire to run away or just check out. When leaders do not maintain themselves, they let down those they serve.

The challenge is to recognize when we need rest, how much we need, and how best to find it. At one point in time, the solution may be a day off. At another point, we may need a week or two of vacation. Periodically, we may need a monthlong sabbatical if we are to avoid long-term ineffectiveness. Guilt, workaholism, and being deemed lazy or wimpy are all burdens that leaders must bear when pursuing legitimate rest and recreation.

Everyone in high, low, and medium roles of leadership must include intentional downtime as a necessary part of making uptime possible. People who are always up, always on, and rarely pull back to renew and refresh are liable to make poor decisions. Leaders must be marathoners more than sprinters. They must pace themselves, and they need to know when to say no in order to maximize their effectiveness. Safeguarding our health, enriching our relationships, replenishing our energy levels, and restoring our souls—this is all just good stewardship. Soulless leadership is dangerous leadership.

LESSON 15

LEADER REST

The importance of rest and renewal

Context

Effective leading is stressful; it eventually depletes energy and causes weariness. Leaders need to discern when they need rest so that they can stay strong for the sake of serving others, even though the rest itself may cause them to feel as if they're shirking their responsibilities. Leaders must learn not to confuse laziness with rest and should also not confuse hectic activities that are unrelated to work with rest. These activities may divert our attention from work, but they don't adequately recharge our batteries.

Discussion

1. What are some signs that you need to rest? What signs have you seen in others?
2. What are some of the challenges of seeking effective rest and renewal?
3. How does our society, and perhaps our church, work against effective resting?
4. How do you distinguish the difference between legitimate rest and laziness?
5. What are some personal, creative ways you've discovered to renew yourself?

Activity 1

Have participants place their chairs in a circle, facing out. Ask them to sit silently and empty their minds for three minutes. Try to make sure the room is totally silent. After three minutes, talk about how difficult it is to shut down in this way. Ask participants what went on in their minds as they tried to concentrate on nothing and why this sort of exercise is so frustrating and may even be considered a waste. You may wish to expand the discussion to include the challenges of consistently setting aside quiet time to pray and be alone with God.

Activity 2

Before the meeting, create a restful atmosphere in your meeting room. Try dimming the lights, playing soothing background music, and lighting scented candles. After everyone has assembled, talk about the importance of rest. Then give everyone fifteen minutes of solitude in which they may read Scriptures, journal their reflections, or write a letter to God. After the experience, ask participants to form groups of three or four and share what they accomplished and what was difficult for them in the fifteen minutes of forced solitude. Finally, ask them to share with people in their groups how they can make rest an intentional part of their lives.

I.N.S.P.E.C.T.

Make sure expectations are met by following up

One of the most important maxims of leadership is, Don't **ex**pect what you don't **in**spect. While leaders tend to be very good at casting vision, they tend to be weak when it comes to execution. How often have you conveyed a great idea to your leadership team only to realize months later that it is no further along? When leaders don't follow up regularly and consistently, associates often become jaded and begin whispering, "Oh, don't worry, the leader will get over this new kick in a few days, and we'll be back to business as usual." All good leaders take accountability seriously by declaring their expectations and developing adequate avenues of inspection. Here's how to do it.

Initiate respectful accountability whenever you establish a new standard or reiterate an old one. By *respectful* accountability, I mean the accountability that avoids the micromanaging, Big Brother attitude of control freaks. Instead, ask, "How can we serve you in accomplishing this? What progress have we made?"

Never confuse inspection with expectation. Your inspections must really measure whether your expectations have been met. Needless forms and processes will fail to produce the outcome you are seeking.

Select what you expect. Don't ask for the world. People can do only so much. Choose a few vital tasks or processes you plan to inspect, then do it. Too much inspection reduces productivity and causes people to lose sight of the big picture.

Performance must be measurable. A lot of things we do may be difficult to measure, to quantify in tangible terms. Come up with performance standards that can be effectively communicated and measured to avoid nebulous, subjective opinions.

Excellence is the goal. Make it clear that improvement, not perfection, is the goal. Make constructive criticism a valued part of your church's culture without diminishing self-esteem and self-confidence.

Celebrate the victories. Party hardy when associates excel and the church really does what it seeks to do. Whoop it up when you make progress.

Take the time to follow up. It's tedious. It can be boring. It can give you a headache. Employ the help of others, but make sure it gets done.

LESSON 16

I.N.S.P.E.C.T.

Make sure expectations are met by following up

Context

It's common for leaders to begin new things, fail to follow up on them, and then become frustrated when they are not accomplished. Many churches have set standards but failed to hold their staffs accountable for meeting them. A leader can't just state a new idea in the form of a policy or announce it once and assume it will become a reality. Don't expect what you don't inspect.

Discussion

1. Can you think of a stated policy in our church that is rarely inspected? Why isn't it inspected?
2. Is this policy still important, or should it be eliminated?
3. If it should be retained, what is an appropriate way to inspect and reinforce it?
4. Think of an example of an objective that would be worth pursuing and an appropriate way to ensure that it is achieved.
5. How can you place a greater emphasis on celebrating accomplishments in your area of responsibility?

Activity 1

Ask one person to volunteer to leave the room, then tell the others that you'd like them to participate in an experiment with behavioral reinforcement. Their goal will be to get the volunteer to enter the room, stand in a far corner of the room, and face the wall, but they won't give him or her any specific instructions to do so. Instead, the group will boo, hiss, or groan when the person moves further from the corner and cheer and applaud when he or she moves toward it. Once the person is standing in the corner, lead the group in a standing ovation. Afterward, explore the reasons that reinforcement is such a strong motivator.

Activity 2

Before the activity, prepare 9x12 envelopes so that you have an envelope for every three to four people. In each envelope put a crayon or marker, an 8½x11-inch sheet of paper, a cassette tape, scissors, a dollar, a quarter, a dime, and a tissue.

Ask participants to form teams of three or four people each, and give each team an envelope. Instruct teams that they will have five minutes to make a beautiful paper airplane but they may only use up to three of the items in the envelope to do so. When time is up, inspect each plane. Remind the group that the goal was to make a "beautiful paper airplane," not necessarily to make the best flying plane. Ask participants which items were useful in achieving the goal and which were not. Use this activity to illustrate how easy it is to perform tasks that may be worthwhile but don't help accomplish a stated outcome. Discuss churches' propensity to inspect the things that are really not most strategic to achieving stated objectives. Brainstorm about ways to begin to inspect what is most important to the church's success.

SWEAT THE SMALL STUFF

The difference between micromanaging and pursuing excellence

"**D**on't sweat the small stuff." This maxim reminds us that it's unhealthy to make a big deal out of a small deal. On the other hand, winners know that it's vital to monitor the minute details that can make a big difference to their success or that of their organization. The difference between Olympic medallists and forgotten competitors can often be measured in hundredths of seconds. Attention to detail is often what separates the winner from tenth place. Our Creator's attention to detail is evident in every aspect of creation, from the intricate balance of the universe to the exquisite points of a snowflake. So how can leaders balance sweating the small stuff with keeping the big picture in focus? The secret is to elevate the importance of detail without micromanaging.

- Micromanaging is about gaining control. Leading is about releasing control.
- Micromanaging strives for perfection. Leading strives for excellence.
- Micromanaging tends to sacrifice the big picture for the small. Leading tends to accomplish the big picture by paying appropriate attention to its components.
- The micromanager assumes that success stems from getting everything right. Leaders recognize that their organizations can get everything right and still fail, but that they will rarely succeed if they don't strive to get things right.

At times, leaders must put on the white gloves and check for dusty furniture. This kind of inspection communicates accountability, models attention to detail, and properly communicates that others ought to do the same. A reputation for being picky is often good, even if it is irritating at times. Leaders who don't care about details are often communicating mediocrity and modeling inattention to excellence. At the same time, leaders must not get bogged down in details; they must trust others to attend to most of them.

Savvy leaders understand the constant pressure to balance the big picture with the small ones. They realize that the struggle to achieve this balance is in itself a sign of health.

OK TO COPY

LESSON 17

SWEAT THE SMALL STUFF

The difference between micromanaging and pursuing excellence

Context

Leaders who pay too much attention to detail waste energy and diminish the scope of their leadership. Those who overlook details often compromise excellence, which in itself limits effectiveness. Leaders must strive to create a culture in which attention to detail is vital but perfectionism is not rewarded and most details are the responsibility of people other than the leader.

Discussion

1. To which details does our church pay too little attention?
2. What would be the benefits of focusing on those details?
3. To what degree should the leaders be involved in this focus?
4. What is your role in ensuring that details receive appropriate attention in our church?
5. How do you communicate the differences between perfectionism and excellence?

Activity 1

As knotwha tyo urcoun try Cand of ory oua skwh aty oucand Of oryou rc ount ry

Write the preceding sentence on a white board, and ask participants to decipher it. (It's a memorable quote from President Kennedy's inaugural address—"Ask not what your country can do for you; ask what you can do for your country."—without attention to details such as punctuation, spacing, spelling, and capitalization.)

Now copy this sentence on a white board and discuss its meaning: *You are the one who will be the one, the one you will be when you wake up.* While the sentence's spelling, capitalization, punctuation, and spacing are correct, the sentence itself is fairly meaningless.

Use these activities to illustrate the fact that too little attention to detail may ruin the impact of something important, while too much attention to the details of an insignificant matter is a waste of resources.

Activity 2

Before this activity, gather blocks of wood and use pencil to draw a simple design or write a phrase, such as "details count," on each.

Form groups of two or three. Give each group a block of wood. Give each group three pieces of sandpaper: very fine, medium, and coarse. If you'd like, you could also throw in a sheet of paper without any grit. Instruct groups to remove the writing or graphic with the paper provided.

Ask which grain worked best and why. Make the point that, although the sand particles are very small, they make a big difference in the results. Ask participants to list some small details that are vital to their areas of responsibility. Ask them to brainstorm ways that leaders—who are often not detail-minded—can ensure these things get done without doing them themselves.

LESSON 18

A LOT OF A LITTLE

Deciphering what information is helpful

Effective leaders seek information that will enable them to make wise decisions. But in this age of information overload, leaders can easily be overwhelmed by a daily bombardment of information. Even so, they can't escape their responsibility to sort through information to detect the fertile truth that will increase their organizations' effectiveness.

Some leaders respond by consuming large quantities of information, assuming that if some is good much is best. They surf the Net, scan a half-dozen newspapers, and heap books and articles on and around their nightstands. Unfortunately, all this information can be like a car headlight in need of adjustment: It shoots its beam into the night air instead of on the road where it is needed.

Other leaders give up altogether. While they may think they're moving to a simpler lifestyle, they are in fact running from the hard work of information sorting. They run the risk of sterile thinking, tunnel vision, and growing incompetence.

Effective leaders are idea gleaners. Jesus said, "The truth will set you free" (John 8:32). The truth he spoke of was specific and spiritual. He did not mean it as so many philosophers have defined it through the years, as generic truth. Any old truth, such as 2 + 2 = 4, does not have the ability to free us, but the right truth does.

One way to discover appropriate sources of information is to talk to people you admire and respect. Ask them what they are reading and where they find their ideas. Make notes, follow up, and see if the sources resonate with you. If not, move on.

Don't rely entirely on information sources that were helpful to you in the past. New books, thinkers, and Web sites are constantly arising. If we lived in a world that changed little from moment to moment, continually gaining new insights would not be necessary. But constantly changing circumstances require continual, selective information harvesting.

The number of information sources that are truly useful in any given context is limited. Read the few books, periodicals, and other sources that keep you informed. Toss the rest. They are a waste of your time, money, and, most of all, clarity of thought. Your goal is to shine a laser beam, not a floodlight, on the professional information available to you.

LESSON 18

A LOT OF A LITTLE

Deciphering what information is helpful

Context

Even though leaders are flooded with information, finding potent ideas is a challenge. In the face of information overload, some leaders try to consume more than they need while others give up entirely. Effective leaders do the work of finding good resources and then they study those resources on a regular basis.

Discussion

1. List two or three great books related to your field that you've read or plan to read in the near future.
2. List one or two quality periodicals related to your work.
3. List two or three of the best work-related Web sites you've discovered.
4. Name three or four sharp leaders who might share their favorite sources of information with you.
5. What is your most pressing challenge in discovering, obtaining, and using information?

Activity 1

Set out a box of construction pieces, such as Legos, that are designed to make a specific toy or structure. Include some extra pieces that are not needed for the structure. Ask your team to use the kit's instructions to construct the item. When the kit is completed, there should be some pieces left over. Ask participants what they did with the extra pieces. Did the presence of the unnecessary pieces slow down construction? If so, how?

Relate this activity to the subject of unnecessary information. Ask participants how they can avoid information that wastes their time and energy and diminishes their effectiveness.

Activity 2

Ask participants to use the upcoming week to determine the top five to seven resources in their areas of responsibility. Ask them to report the names of the people they contacted, as well as the titles of books, periodicals, newsletters, Web sites, and other sources. Sharing resources with peers is often amazingly productive.

LESSON

19 FIREFIGHTING

Effective ways to handle criticism

Responding to criticism is an inescapable part of leading. Like fire, criticism can work for you or against you. The difference is in how you respond to it. Here are four rules to help you avoid being burned by criticism.

1. Expect criticism to be a part of the job. Sometimes we are thrown off-balance by criticism because we unconsciously believe that criticism should be rare and even non-existent. President Truman liked to say, "If you can't stand the heat, get out of the kitchen." I like to say, "If you can't create some heat, get out of the kitchen." Leaders exist to initiate improvement and change, which will usually result in friction, and that friction will often give rise to criticism. If you haven't been criticized for some time, question your leading. Also understand that leaders are often the focal point of their organizations and will therefore attract much of the criticism.

2. Look for the grain of truth. When rainmakers try to create precipitation, they seed clouds, knowing that water will often collect around a particle of dust until it becomes heavy enough to fall. While even the slightest drop of criticism might be nearly all water, assume there's a particle of truth in it. Identifying this truth will give you an opportunity to improve. The particle may be a tiny part of the entire criticism, but don't let that cause you to deny its presence. Obviously, if there are larger truths involved, you would do well to listen, ask related questions, and take the criticism to heart.

3. Consider the source. If you value all criticism equally, you'll endanger the church, not to mention your self-image. After a certain amount of time in leadership, you'll learn to identify chronic naysayers, self-appointed experts, and well-meaning pessimists. Some people's criticisms are more of a plea for help and attention than an expression of legitimate concern. Consider lightly, if at all, anonymous comments, because they are usually irresponsible and do not allow you to weigh the quality of the source. Scattered, random, lone criticisms often are more personal than organizational. But if you begin hearing a few independent critiques along the same theme, you should investigate them. On the other hand, don't be overwhelmed if someone says, "Everyone's feeling this way." Most people's social circles comprise five to fifteen people. Chances are they meant to say, "A couple of my friends have talked about this issue with me."

If the critic is a proven ally, listen more intently. Scripture tells us that the criticism of a friend is more valuable than the compliment of an enemy (Proverbs 27:6).

4. Respond appropriately. There's no need to hunt gophers with a

 FIREFIGHTING

bazooka. Conversely, shooting an attacking lion with a water pistol is equally foolish. When you begin to bristle, choose instead to smile, listen, and respond simply, "That's interesting. Let me consider that. Thanks for your concern." Walk off and avoid saying something that will require significantly more cleanup than is necessary. Leaders often harm themselves by overreacting or responding emotionally.

Because of your influence, your response is important. By deferring a response or saying, "You know what? This is not a good time to talk. Can we set up an appointment when I can give you the quality time you deserve?" you put yourself in the driver's seat and allow yourself time to gear up mentally, emotionally, and spiritually. Every leader is a firefighter. Don't run from fires, but learn not to burn.

FIREFIGHTING

Effective ways to handle criticism

Context

Leaders can't avoid being criticized, and that fact alone is one reason many people refuse to take on leadership roles. After leaders accept the inevitability of criticism, they must learn to respond appropriately to it, as their responses to criticism will quickly reveal their mettle. Running from criticism and attacking critics are equally destructive responses that do little to help leaders or those they serve.

Discussion

1. For you, what is the most difficult aspect of dealing with criticism?

2. What personal technique works well for you when you are criticized?

3. Think of someone who seems to handle criticism well. Describe what makes this person effective.

4. What is your immediate, internal reaction to criticism? Have you developed any tools to prevent this response from hampering your dedication to your leadership role?

5. How important is it to consider the source when weighing the value of criticism? Discuss the "everybody feels this way" tactic that some people use to fortify their opinions.

Activity 1

Choose four volunteers to participate in a role-play. (Two people will be on each team, thereby lessening the stress that an individual might feel playing a role alone.) Explain that two of the participants are directors of the church nursery. They've enacted some new check-in policies in an effort to improve security. The other two participants are volunteers who disagree with the new practices. Their complaints are important to them, but the nursery directors are committed to the new practices for the sake of the children and parents. Ask the four participants to spend three minutes role-playing the situation in a way that demonstrates how *not* to handle criticism. Then ask them to spend three minutes role-playing in a way that demonstrates a constructive response to criticism. Finally, spend three or four minutes dissecting the techniques used in the role-play.

Activity 2

Before this activity, find four or five small boxes, such as jewelry or gift boxes, and place various items of varying weight in them. One might be very light, one very heavy, and the other three in between. Ask one person to act as a human scale by standing with arms stretched out from the sides, palms up. Tell the other team members that their goal is to balance the boxes on the arms so that the "scale" is balanced.

Use this activity to demonstrate that each source of feedback does not necessarily carry the same weight as others and that certain people provide more valuable input than others. For example, the criticism of a person who is consistently negative should be taken more lightly than that of a friend. Discuss how to weigh opinions differently, without dismissing helpful feedback from people who may not be likable.

LESSON 20

"GOOD ENOUGH" NEVER IS

The pursuit of perpetual improvement

During times of stability and slow change, you might create a quality product, service, or experience and keep it unchanged with positive results. But in dynamic, quickly changing times, yesterday's good is today's mediocre and tomorrow's poor. The pursuit of excellence is a perpetual process. The cycle of creation, evaluation, improvement, and re-evaluation is relentless.

In the Bible, the first mention of quality evaluation is in Genesis, when God considered what he had created and "saw that it was good." Factories that never inspect their widgets, airlines that never ask passengers their opinions, and churches that pretend that all is well are likely to quickly become outdated or irrelevant. Head-in-sand denial may provide temporary relief, but it leads to long-term pain. Excellence is more a process than an outcome. Leaders who build constant-improvement systems into their organizations can expect to produce continually better products and services.

The pursuit of excellence should not be confused with the pursuit of perfection. Perfection focuses on what is wrong, whereas excellence pursues what is better. Perfection tends to be obsessive and may fail to consider whether the improvement is worth the added cost. Excellence recognizes the point of diminishing returns, when further improvement is not worth the added cost. People are motivated by the pursuit of excellence, but they are discouraged by the pursuit of perfection.

Although it may not be the leader's job to perform the task of evaluation, he or she must be sure that it takes place. Leaders are human and tend to think that things are better than they really are. The pursuit of perpetual improvement must be intentional if it is to be at all.

Remember that leaders are social architects. They must be able to read and influence the culture. You can put your hands on your hips and say, "I don't like this. I'm not going to do this." When you take that stand, though, you resign as a leader. Righteous idealists make good prophets but lousy leaders. Our culture mandates that we keep an eye on quality, pursue excellence, and evaluate constantly.

Pastors should always be asking, "Who is the church? When did we last ask our congregants for feedback? Do we do exit interviews with former attendees? Do we ask new visitors to give us their first impressions, and do we reward them or provide incentives for them to do so?" Although a shot of truth can sting a bit, it can also inoculate us against the potentially fatal disease of mediocrity.

LESSON 20

"GOOD ENOUGH" NEVER IS

The pursuit of perpetual improvement

Context

In the midst of striving just to keep pace with life and the mandates of leadership, leaders must beware of the tendency of mediocrity to gradually creep into even the best of churches. The pursuit of excellence must be a constant, conscious endeavor. Leaders must champion improvement and excellence. Effective leaders don't fully delegate this responsibility.

Discussion

1. How do we assess quality in our church and specifically in your area of responsibility?
2. What tools do we use to gather feedback from team members and the congregation?
3. How can we do a better job of measuring excellence? How can we get tangible information about intangible matters?
4. To what degree is it the leader's role to raise the standard of excellence?
5. How can leaders avoid getting caught up in the details of quality improvement?

Activity 1

Ask participants to form groups of three to five. Tell participants they are members of an elite group of experts who are responsible for designing improvements to everyday items. Each group will have five minutes to brainstorm about improvements to the item you give to it. Distribute items such as an umbrella or a toilet paper dispenser. After five minutes have elapsed, ask someone from each group to explain the group's ideas. Finally, discuss the process of evaluating commonplace practices and striving to improve them.

Activity 2

Before this activity, write "X" on one slip of paper. Add this slip to a bowl containing enough blank slips of paper for all participants to have one. Gather three clear glasses full of water, a spoon, a spoonful of dirt, and a few dead insects.

To begin the activity, say, "One of you has chosen a slip of paper with an X on it. Here is your assignment: You represent a congregant or a potential congregant." Line up the three glasses of water and say, "Here are three glasses of water. In one, I'll put just a little bit of dirt, not much, not enough to hurt you." Stir a teaspoon of soil into the water, then say, "In this glass I'll put a couple of small bugs; they are minute compared to the amount of water in the glass." Drop in a dead insect, then say, "Now, the person representing a current or potential churchgoer has to drink from one of these glasses." Unless the person is a joker, he or she will choose the clean water.

Use this analogy to show how people choose among competing alternatives. Church leaders often excuse their flaws or missteps by saying, "Our church is just a little flawed. We make so few mistakes compared to everything we do right. People won't see the mistakes, and if they do, they'll overlook them. We can get away with it."

A SIGHT FOR SORE EYES

The role and importance of vision

Perhaps the biggest single difference between leaders and managers is that leaders possess a vision for the future of their organization. A leader is a social artist who paints portraits of the future. People come to enjoy and critique these works of art, and they'll buy those they enjoy most. Where there is insufficient vision, the people languish. Vision gives leaders purpose beyond a paycheck, unction to get to the junction, and the umph to triumph.

In leaders such as Moses, Jesus, Napoleon, Gandhi, Abraham Lincoln, and Martin Luther King, Jr., history reveals that visionary movements start with visionary leaders. I have yet to see a vision hatch from a committee's egg. Even among groups in which cooperation is highly valued, key individuals must continually cast the vision and passionately involve others in maintaining it.

Surveys help us understand priorities and felt needs, revealing what sort of vision will gain the most support. Planning and goal-setting help us monitor progress toward turning vision into reality. Brainstorming sessions help us think strategically and creatively. But none of these activities are substitutes for vision itself. Vision gives us not only the *what* but also the *why*. It engages our emotions, not just our minds. It oozes with hope and thrives on the intangible workings of the will. A mission statement is a value statement describing the basic intention of an organization. A vision statement is a color snapshot of what that mission will look like when it is realized.

A vision may be measured on the basis of three factors: urgency ("We must do it now, or we'll lose this opportunity."), importance ("If we don't do this, life will not be as meaningful."), and size ("How big do you want to dream?"). Rank each factor on a scale of one to five, with one representing nonexistent and five representing powerful. Add the rankings of all three factors together. If the total is one to five, you can ask, "What vision?" Visions with totals of six to ten will be noticed, but they may get lost in the array of other matters vying for attention. Visions with scores over ten are the ones that will be noticed and will have the greatest impact.

Whether you are a leader of a small or large church, consider the importance of having a vision for it. Churches that lack vision have a hard time keeping talented people, motivating employees, and serving people.

LESSON 21

A SIGHT FOR SORE EYES

The role and importance of vision

Context

Vision is enormously important to the success of every church. Whether you're the leader of a Fortune 500 company or recruiting volunteers for the church nursery, your vision for your area of responsibility will largely determine your success. The vision cast by a leader inspires and engages the imaginations of those he or she leads. One challenge is to find tangible ways to measure such an intangible concept.

Discussion

1. Think of a visionary leader you've heard or followed. What was it about this person that made you want to commit to the task at hand?
2. What is your vision for your area of responsibility? If you do not have one, why do you think you don't need one? Why is having a vision helpful and strategic?
3. What do you think about the three components of a strong vision: urgency, importance, and size? Assess the unique role of each.
4. How can you consistently communicate the vision of your church? (Don't limit your ideas to a charismatic, motivational speaker.)
5. Discuss the difference between goals and visions.

Activity 1

Procure a written, audio, or video copy of a famous speech in which a vision was articulated, such as Martin Luther King, Jr.'s, "I have a dream" speech or President Kennedy's speech about the Peace Corps or landing a man on the moon. Ask participants to analyze the speech to determine what made it so effective in engendering commitment and long-term results.

Activity 2

Ask each participant to write a vision statement for the church or the area he or she leads. Ask everyone to determine how the vision measures up in terms of urgency, importance, and size. Ask how it can be improved. Challenge participants to consider how they can cast their visions to engage the hearts and minds of those they influence in a variety of ways.

LESSON

THE GOLDILOCKS SYNDROME

Becoming aware of comfort zones

Remember your first kiss? Mine was a quick peck on the cheek from Debra Ann Waddingham as I was getting off the school bus in elementary school. What a kiss! Do you remember your first job? How about your first house or your first day of school or the birth of your first child? First experiences can be exhilarating, but they can also be scary. Fear causes us to shy away from changes and new experiences.

Nearly every thermostat has a range called the comfort zone. This is the temperature range in which most people feel comfortable—not too hot, not too cold...juuuuust right. But the Goldilocks Syndrome can thwart creativity and productivity more than any other single influence. It is a strong, natural desire to seek comfort zones, places where we feel at home, in an effort to avoid a natural fear of the unknown.

There are two kinds of firsts: involuntary and voluntary. Involuntary firsts are experiences into which we are thrust and include experiences such as an unplanned child or a new role at work. We react to involuntary firsts. Voluntary firsts, on the other hand, are the result of proactive efforts.

Leaders try to be proactive. They voluntarily pursue first experiences because they know that comfort zones can engender a deceptive sense of security. They know that long-term comfort can produce even longer-term discomfort. They recognize that strategic decisions that lead to short-term discomfort are often necessary for long-term health. This movement out of a comfort zone is intentional. Leaders learn to feel comfortable with ambiguity as their natural fear of first experiences becomes a familiar friend.

Assume that you, your team, and your church are in a comfort zone unless you can show that you are not. Comfort zones tend to lull us into a false sense of well-being. Just as bath water eventually matches the ambient temperature of the room, our goals and work patterns can become lukewarm if left undisturbed.

Scriptures tell us that our Creator is constantly doing new things. "See, the former things have taken place, and new things I declare" (Isaiah 42:9). When is the last time you voluntarily did something new? When was the last time your church took a risk, moved beyond traditions and norms, pushed the envelope?

If you plan to stay in your comfort zone, you're human, but you're probably not a leader. Comfort zones are fine until they threaten productivity and effectiveness. In the face of so much change, society cries out for more and better leaders. Ironically, it also clings blindly to the comfort of old, ineffective methods. Face your fears; turn up the thermostat.

LESSON 22

THE GOLDILOCKS SYNDROME

Becoming aware of comfort zones

Context

Leaders must be the first to confront the tendency of teams and congregations to seek and stay in comfort zones. They must recognize their own natural fear of the unknown and understand this fear in others. At the same time, they must become comfortable with change. They must challenge others to move out of their comfort zones to remain effective.

Discussion

1. Do you remember your first kiss? When and where did it take place? Who bestowed it?
2. When did you last try a new restaurant or a new item from a menu?
3. Why do you think we're prone to seek comfort zones?
4. Do you think you and/or your team may be in a comfort zone? Why or why not?
5. What can leaders do to move their teams out of comfort zones?

Activity 1

An hour or so before the participants enter the meeting room, either turn up the heat as high as it will go or set the air conditioning on its lowest setting. Make sure that no one adjusts the thermostat.

After everyone has arrived, begin the lesson and then let the conversation gravitate to discussion of the room's temperature. Allow this to lead into a discussion about people's various responses to discomfort. Compare this experience to others that create anxiety and irritability and demand leaders to respond.

Activity 2

After participants are seated, ask everyone to change places with someone else. You might even stipulate that people of a certain age sit together, that people with the same hair color sit together, or that people sit together because of some other arbitrary criteria. You might do this once or twice again. (Your goal is to create frustration stemming from change.) When things have settled down, talk about the emotional aspect of change. Compare the emotions stirred up by this trivial activity with those engendered by organizational changes that require people to move out of their comfort zones.

23 SACRED COWS

Taking an honest look at traditions

Do you know why train tracks are the width they are? Because train cars were designed to be the same width as horse-drawn carriages, which in turn were designed to fit into the ruts created by ancient Roman chariots. The letters and symbols on computer keyboards are arranged as they are because, when typewriters were first developed, early typists could pound the keys so fast the machines would jam. A more difficult keyboard arrangement, developed in 1873, caused typists to type at a pace the typewriter could handle. Our lives are full of daily and weekly activities that have more to do with habit and tradition than with relevance and effectiveness. We are creatures of habit.

Undoubtedly, your church has an array of practices that have outlived their effectiveness. We perpetuate these practices because "we've always done it that way." Even new churches, which are often born from a desire to escape ineffectual traditions, create their own traditions that will eventually become just as unproductive. When Moses was on the mountain, talking to God and receiving the Ten Commandments, the people of Israel asked Aaron to create a golden calf to represent God in their midst. Their problem was that they began to worship the image instead of God.

Images, rituals, practices, and even physical equipment and structures often assume more importance than they deserve. When pastors allow their parishioners to hold on to meaningless traditions and unproductive practices, they do a disservice to the church as well as those they serve. To keep their organizations healthy, effective leaders expose sacred cows for what they are. Remember the title of Bill Easum's 1995 book: *Sacred Cows Make Gourmet Burgers.*

The first step is to recognize sacred cows: practices or things that are of little benefit but are considered above criticism. The next step is to analyze the sacred cow. How did it get started? What harm does it do? What good does it prevent? Who will be offended if it is butchered? The next step is to create a dismantling strategy. You may need to employ drastic action, or you may simply emphasize something more creative or effective. The final step is to assess when the new practices that replaced the sacred cows have become sacred cows themselves. because agents of change are often capable of identifying the sacred cows of others while remaining blind to their own.

LESSON 23

SACRED COWS

Taking an honest look at traditions

Context

I once heard someone say that "tradition is the faith of the dead; traditionalism is dead faith." Change-oriented people run the risk of being bored with anything that is redundant, regardless of its effectiveness. But most of us invest in rituals that have outlived their effectiveness. Leaders need to be on the prowl for organizational traditions that have become a part of the culture but have lost their relevance and fruitfulness.

Discussion

1. What is a sacred cow that you've identified in another organization?
2. How does it hurt the organization? How did it become institutionalized?
3. Which of your practices may be sacred cows?
4. Are they productive? Why or why not?
5. What can we do in our church to address traditions that have outlived their usefulness in order to pursue more effective habits and practices?

Activity 1

Before the meeting, write the alphabet on self-stick notes, one letter per note. Arrange the notes on a white board as if they were on a computer keyboard.

When participants arrive, form groups of two to four, and ask groups to think about how to rearrange the keyboard in order to make it more efficient. After groups have brainstormed, discuss their recommendations. Explain that the letters and symbols on computer keyboards are arranged as they are because, when typewriters were first developed, early typists could pound the keys so fast the machines would jam. A more difficult keyboard arrangement, developed in 1873, caused typists to type at a pace the typewriter could handle. Apply this insight to practices in your church that may have outlived their usefulness.

Activity 2

Before this session, draw an outline of a cow on an 8½ x11-inch sheet of paper. Make a photocopy for each participant.

Give everyone a cow outline, and ask participants to each describe one sacred cow, tradition, or ritual that they have identified in their areas of responsibility. Then ask them to write down how the practice originated and why it was important. Finally, ask them to describe a new, more relevant practice that could achieve the same important goal more effectively. The goal is not to toss something just because it has endured, but to identify that which has endured but has become ineffectual.

24 WAG THE DOG

How perception can affect the ability to lead

People do not respond to reality; they respond to their perception of reality. For example, let's say you come home to a dark house. Before you reach the light switch, you think you see something move in the room. Adrenaline shoots through your body. "Is it a person? Am I being robbed? Am I going to be attacked?" You strike your best Bruce Lee pose, flip on the switch, and see...nothing. Nothing is there, but your body and nervous system responded to the perceived threat.

When you translate this concept into leadership, you begin to understand why perceptions, whether or not they are based on truth, play an important role in your ability to lead. If a leader is perceived to be fearful, spiteful, negative, or ignorant, people will respond as if he or she is until they are shown otherwise.

The problem with perceptions is that they are not always grounded in truth. No one has all the information necessary for an objective understanding of the truth, so we tend to fill in the blanks with our guesses. Many of those guesses are based on perceptions, especially since people are often too intimidated to simply ask leaders to explain their views. If people's perceptions of their leaders are negative, they'll assume that those leaders are motivated by negative impulses. Countless leaders throughout history have lost their power and influence because of gossip, bad public relations, or underestimating the importance of perception.

Of course, the best way to manage perceptions is to remain ethical and to maintain wholesome, healthy attitudes. But a leader is also smart to avoid the *appearance* of evil. This may mean communicating your motives rather than assuming that people know them. It may mean avoiding something that in itself is not wrong but may be construed as shady. (Joseph was certainly a pure-hearted young man, but by being alone with Potiphar's wife, he unwittingly set himself up for trouble.) The pressure of the limelight can certainly wear on a conscientious leader, but those who ignore it often do not last long in leadership.

Savvy leaders are not the ones with superior publicists. They are the ones who consider these questions before they act: How might this appear to others? Is this worth the risk of being misunderstood? How can I do this without raising eyebrows or questions? What might be the downside if I say this? Am I doing my best to prevent disgrace and innuendo from infecting my leadership?

LESSON 24

WAG THE DOG

How perception can affect the ability to lead

Context

Leaders can't avoid being judged by those who would follow them, but they are often judged less on their *actual* motives and attitudes than on others' *perceptions* of their motives and attitudes. Raising awareness of the importance of perception is often sufficient to cause leaders to avoid reckless behavior.

Discussion

1. Can you think of a leader who lost his or her ability to lead because of negative perceptions?
2. Were these perceptions based on reality, false assumptions, or both? How do you know?
3. Describe some examples of actions or statements that may adversely affect perceptions of a leader.
4. "I don't care what people think of me." Is a leader who utters these words being boldly wise or naively foolish?
5. How can you care about perceptions without living in fear of what people will say or caring so much that your leadership is distorted?

Activity 1

Play the old-fashioned game Telephone to illustrate how distorted a leader's remarks may become through constant repetition. Hand one person a piece of paper with a message written on it. For example, write, "We are going to be rewarding those who get this right." Instruct that person to whisper the statement, one time only, into the ear of the person next to him or her. The second person will then whisper the statement to the next person and so on. The very last person to receive the message will stand and say what he or she heard.

Use this activity to lead into a discussion of the effects of gossip, innuendo, and false impressions on leaders and churches.

Activity 2

Before this activity, write the following quotation, with the different attributions, on slips of paper, one quote and attribution per slip. Form groups of three or four people each, and give each group a slip of paper. (The groups won't realize that the quote has been attributed differently in each group.)

"People are the root of all that is good and bad."—Adolf Hitler

"People are the root of all that is good and bad."—Robert Kennedy

"People are the root of all that is good and bad."—Billy Graham

"People are the root of all that is good and bad."—Elton John

"People are the root of all that is good and bad."—Mother Teresa

Give members of each group three minutes to discuss their opinions of the quote. Then inform everyone that the quote is fictitious and the attributions are false. Ask groups how their perceptions of the sources influenced their views. Discuss the importance of positive perceptions to effective leadership.

(Be sure to gather and dispose of all the slips of paper to avoid potential misperceptions!)

LEADER INSURANCE

When things go wrong

How should a leader respond when something goes awry, a staff member creates a scandal, a big event goes bust, or a pet project fails? First, the leader must find a solution. Then he or she must control the damage by making sure that misperceptions, byproducts, and the aftermath of the problem do not do additional harm.

Doctors know that a minor cut left unattended can result in infection and gangrene. While it is dangerous to overreact to a problem, it is also foolish to be unconcerned about its ripple effects. Leaders must assess the real damage as well as the problems that might arise from it. When military and disaster experts strategize, they consider a variety of situations, including worst-case scenarios. As a leader, you should do similar assessments at least mentally and sometimes with others.

Scriptures tell us to count the costs before acting (see Luke 14:28-32). This advice is useful not only in regard to new projects, but also in regard to continuing commitments. For example, you might want to ignore a complaint you hear from a chronic complainer. But if that person interprets your response to mean that you are uncaring or negligent and decides to tell other team members his or her feelings, you'll face a problem that's bigger than the original complaint. When a staff member leaves for less than perfect reasons, should you throw a farewell party or make a public announcement explaining the situation? Each decision will create a different outcome.

More than likely, you can think of instances in which a small event turned into a big deal because it was mishandled or ignored. Try to get firsthand facts about an event if you were not directly involved. Determine how people might misread the circumstances and overreact. Consider the social networks of those involved or offended. (The stronger and larger the networks, the more important it is to be concerned.) Sometimes the best way to determine an appropriate response is to make a phone call or arrange an informal, face-to-face meeting with those involved. It's also helpful to look for a trusted friend who can offer advice and an insider's perspective.

A good leader will take steps to provide something like an insurance policy. As you confront problems and difficult situations, you try to insure the health and welfare of the church. While you cannot avoid all damage, you can strive to reduce the kind of damage that is apt to arise through either neglect or overreaction.

LESSON

LEADER INSURANCE

When things go wrong

Context

It is just as important for leaders to anticipate and defuse a problem's potential aftermath as it is to respond appropriately to the problem itself. Avoiding intentional damage control can cause leaders to magnify the negative impact of a relatively minor event.

Discussion

1. Can you think of a problem that arose from a relatively minor event?
2. What are the challenges of anticipating a problem's fallout?
3. How can haphazard damage control lead to the appearance of a cover-up?
4. Can you think of a situation in which the collateral damage was appropriately controlled?
5. What is a current concern that might require some type of damage control?

Activity 1

Create a model of a beach by placing sand, a few rocks, and perhaps a paper house in a large, shallow pan. Then add water so that it looks like a miniature lake or ocean.

To begin the activity, ask participants to watch carefully as you drop a rock in the water. Chances are, the waves will wash away some of the sand and perhaps damage or destroy the paper house. Discuss the difference between the initial event (the rock hitting the water) and the collateral damage (the waves that ruined the beach and house). Use this to illustrate how the ripple effects of a problem can do more damage than the problem itself. Brainstorm ways to prevent this kind of situation in your church.

Activity 2

Draw a line across a sheet of 8½x11 paper about a quarter or a third of the way from the edge. Using a match or lighter, light one of the corners furthest from the line. Try to do a "controlled burn" so that the fire does not cross the line. (You might give everyone a chance to try this. Be sure to have a metal trash can on hand to catch the burning paper.) Use this activity to lead into a discussion of the need to minimize the reach of problems that crop up in your church.

DISAPPOINTED BY PEOPLE

The leader's responsibility when individuals fail

H ave you ever been let down by someone? Negative leaders tend to doubt people and often find their doubts realized. In their minds, people are lazy, flaky, and prone to drop the ball with little remorse. On the other hand, positive leaders understand that when people fail them, the leaders themselves usually own part of the blame. Thus, the failure of others is a humbling catalyst for leaders to improve their leadership.

Here are seven ways leaders contribute to others' failure:

1. Poor communication. Never assume that because something is clear to you, it's clear to others. Frequently solicit feedback to ensure that you're communicating clearly.

2. Inadequate resources. It's the leader's responsibility to make sure team members have the tools they need to succeed. When someone fails, ask yourself if he or she was properly equipped.

3. Improper accountability. Many leaders don't enjoy following through on projects and checking up on those they lead, but it is absolutely vital to do both in order to ensure the success of the church and the long-term motivation of its people.

4. Inadequate team-building. Ask if those you lead are a group of individuals or a single-minded team. There is a significant difference. The leader's job is to build teams, not just to recruit members.

5. Poor matches. There are no wrong people, just wrong positions. Ask yourself if you've put people in positions that match their strengths, gifts, and passions, places where they can excel.

6. Inadequate training. Anyone can fail without proper preparation—including you—so make sure those you lead receive the right training before you expect them to accomplish a task.

7. Poor team selection. Nearly as important as matching people with positions is creating unified, complementary teams whose members enjoy each other and get along.

Even the best of leaders can't transform everyone. After all, even Jesus had a Judas. But leaders should always ask how they are responsible when others fail. Asking this question prevents futile finger-pointing and unproductive complaining. When people fail you, chances are you've failed them as their leader. Effective leaders ask, "What could I have done to help my people succeed?" So enjoy a slice of humble pie when others fail and use the experience to determine how it can propel you into more effective leading.

LESSON 26

DISAPPOINTED BY PEOPLE

The leader's responsibility when individuals fail

Context

Leaders are human. Like most people, they are tempted to blame others when people or projects fail. Because leaders are ultimately responsible for their churches, they must assess their role in its failures. Perhaps they were responsible for inadequate accountability, poor training, unclear communication, or faulty people selection. When team members fail, the leader fails as well and should use the experience to improve.

Discussion

1. When did someone on your team fail?
2. What was this person's part in the failure? What was the leader's part? Which of the seven weaknesses might have contributed to the failure?
3. Why is it difficult for leaders to recognize and/or admit their responsibility when those they lead do not succeed?
4. What is a realistic way to admit appropriate responsibility when discussing a team failure?
5. What can you do to better prepare your people to succeed?

Activity 1

Choose one person to be a basketball-team coach (or you can be the coach). Then select five people to be on the team. Denote one wall as the basket, and then assign individuals to their positions, but be sure to assign the wrong person to each position. For example, two shorter people are usually guards and play away from the basket. Two taller people are usually placed closer to the basket, on the left and right. Usually, the tallest, strongest person is in the middle, close to and in front of the basket. (If you're meeting in a large room or gym and want to add an extra dimension to this activity, recruit a second team, place its members in the right positions, and then run a play or two to see what happens.)

After assigning the players to the wrong positions, ask everyone to offer an opinion about this setup. Most who know something about the sport will quickly point out the misalignment. Discuss the importance of assigning people to positions that match their strengths and minimize their weaknesses.

Activity 2

Place an open carton of eggs and supplies such as tape, wrapping paper, and bubble wrap on a table. Form teams of two or three, and say, "You've been selected to take part in a special design team whose job is to develop a process for preventing eggs from breaking when dropped from a height of ten to twelve feet. You have three minutes to prepare your egg for the drop. Go."

When time is up, have each team take its egg to a person standing on a chair. This person will hold each egg above his or her head and drop it into a wastebasket. After all the eggs have been dropped, discuss leadership elements that affected the outcome of this assignment. Was a leader needed on each team? Why or why not? How could the process have been improved?

SETTING THE SAIL

The importance of modeling a positive attitude

"**I**t's not the wind that determines the direction of a boat, but the set of the sail." Likewise, attitude, even more than resources, can determine the success or failure of any endeavor. Leaders often forget their ongoing responsibility to emphasize the positive. Even though they are as susceptible to negativity as anyone else, leaders can't afford to convey their own fears and concerns. They don't have the right or the privilege to be an open book when doing so contaminates the atmosphere and endangers the welfare of the church.

Focusing on the good does not mean denying risk. Leaders who exhibit a not-a-cloud-in-the-sky, Pollyanna attitude in the middle of a downpour will lose credibility. But you can face reality without concluding that failure is around the corner. A savvy leader identifies challenges and then expresses reasons for hope in spite of stormy forecasts.

Remember that leaders' words and attitudes are magnified among the people they lead. We're all human, but leaders who ask their people and churches to provide therapy groups for their own insecurities have abdicated leadership. Share your fears with God, a trusted friend outside the church, or a mentor, but don't make your fears a part of your leadership style. When investors hear that the CEO is selling his stock in the company, they're likely to do the same. People under your leadership are investing in you. They are counting on the value of the stock rising.

Even while in prison, the Apostle Paul encouraged his friends to hope. He showed how his imprisonment had given him an inroad into the political and legal system of Rome, enabling him to spread the gospel message. Every situation has negatives and positives. Leaders become leaders by conveying hope. When you're tempted to express a doubt, bite your tongue. Look for the good in each situation. Elevate the positive. Fan the flames of hope. You may not win every game, but your job is to maximize your team's potential. Expressing your doubts and fears depletes that potential. Give hope a chance. Smile. Verbalize the positive or keep quiet.

✓OK TO COPY

LESSON 27

SETTING THE SAIL

The importance of modeling a positive attitude

Context

A leader's verbal and nonverbal cues strongly influence the entire church. When leaders point to the negative or communicate their own fears, they do a disservice to everyone under their leadership. By elevating the positive, leaders impart hope and help others deal with their own fears and doubts. The result is a positive place to work, serve, and experience community.

Discussion

1. Think of a leader you know who consistently faces difficult situations with faith and hope. What makes this person attractive to follow?
2. What is a current problem or challenge you face in your area of responsibility? What are the pessimists in the group saying about it? What are optimistic aspects of the problem that you can emphasize?
3. How can you speak hopefully of a truth that is not positive?
4. What have you learned about controlling your own feelings of doubt and fear for the sake of the team?
5. Why is elevating the positive so important, and when is it needed most?

Activity 1

Turn off all the lights in your meeting room, and use a flashlight or candle to provide enough light so that one person can write. Tell the group that the lights have just gone out and no electricity will be available for four hours. Tell participants to forget about generators and troubleshooting and, instead, to spend the next five minutes brainstorming what they can do to maximize the next four hours. Ask them to list the potential benefits of the situation.

At the end of the brainstorming session, ask participants to think of other situations of this sort that arise continually. Ask them to give examples of how leaders help by focusing on the positive.

Activity 2

Form two teams. Place a minus sign in front of one team and a plus sign in front of the other. Tell participants that both teams will be given the same scenario and will have two minutes to discuss and write down realistic, potential outcomes or side effects of the situation. The team with the minus sign will develop a pessimistic list of possible outcomes. The team with the plus sign will develop an optimistic list.

Here is the situation: "Offerings have been down over the last six months, and the church has to make some significant decisions regarding ministry budgets, staffing, and facility expenses. You must respond to this situation in preparation for the upcoming strategic plan." After two minutes have elapsed, ask the negative team to present its list, then ask the positive team to do the same.

After the presentations, ask the participants to share their emotional responses to the two lists. Explore practical ways that leaders can cultivate hope when it is needed most, during difficult situations.

28 MISSION POSSIBLE

Developing a meaningful mission statement

Mission statements have been in vogue in recent years, but without built-in accountability checks, mission statements have little value. In fact, we are not about what we *say*; we are about what we *do*. For example, companies may say they are service-oriented when, in fact, their employees are rude to customers. Churches proclaim that they exist to help people find God, but many congregations rarely see a new believer in their midst.

We need to do more than define our mission; we also need to insert some sort of painful accountability check to increase the likelihood that we will actually do what we say is important. Without the accountability check, we can too easily believe we are what we say we are. Unfortunately, dysfunctional organizations are as plentiful as dysfunctional people. The problem is not that organizations have problems; the problem is that we deceive ourselves into believing that they don't. The danger is in the lie. We'd much rather perpetuate what we're doing than ask if we're hitting the target.

Identifying the discrepancies between our stated missions and our actual missions helps us see what needs to change. One way to identify these discrepancies is to ask someone we can trust to tell the truth. These truth-tellers may come from within the organization, or they may come from outside. (Outside consultants are often more effective because, when we pay someone to tell us what needs to change, the pain of paying can be enough to motivate us to implement the suggested changes.) In any case, if we don't create a system to help us respond to our need for change, chances are we won't.

People aren't likely to change until their discomfort is acute. Savvy leaders sometimes induce a desire to change by creating situations that introduce pain. For example, leaders might reduce budgets in areas that haven't experienced growth or lay off staff who consistently fall short of expectations. While we're all averse to pain, leaders understand that it can be their best friend when they're striving to move from the status quo.

Define your organization's purpose, then ask yourself if it is achieving it. Ask if its actual priorities match its stated priorities. Ask how you might be fooling yourself into thinking your church is better off than it is. Is truth-telling allowed? What sort of discomfort or pain can you create or allow that will help the church change?

Jesus said his mission in life was to do the will of his Father; it was his food (John 4:34; 6:38). What is your mission? How vital is it in determining your daily tasks? Every organization needs a mission, but just as important is an accountability system that helps to ensure that the mission is being accomplished.

LESSON 28

MISSION POSSIBLE

Developing a meaningful mission statement

Context

What we say and what we do are often quite different. The recent emphasis on mission statements is only worthwhile if we develop systems that hold us accountable to those statements. When we fail to do what we say is important to do, we deceive ourselves and become less effective and credible.

Discussion

1. What is the mission of your area of responsibility?

2. How do you know whether your mission statement is aligned with your day-to-day activities? What measurements are in place?

3. How often do you refer to your mission statement during planning, budgeting, and effectiveness assessments?

4. Do you need to change your mission statement to reflect what you're really doing, or do you need to change what you're doing to reflect your mission statement?

5. What are some "thorns" you can build into your mission statement so that it will hurt when you are not doing what you say is important?

Activity 1

Before the activity, gather board games, one for every four to six participants. Try to find games that most people will not have played, and remove the instructions.

Form teams of four to six people each. Give each team a board game, and tell everyone to begin playing. After five minutes have elapsed, discuss the experience. When no one knew the directions (equivalent to the mission), what was the result? When one or two knew but the others didn't, what was the result? Discuss how this relates to an absence of a clear mission statement in a church. Discuss the role a mission statement plays in giving direction and holding people accountable.

Activity 2

Give everyone a sheet of paper. Then tell participants they have two minutes in which to write down what they believe is the church's mission. (Sharing is not allowed.) Gather the papers, and read the statements aloud. Chances are, people's responses will vary significantly. Discuss how this lack of consensus may affect the achievement of the church's goals and blur the leadership team's focus.

If you have time, delve further into this topic by writing your church's mission statement on a white board. Then compare the church's goals and budgets and the leadership team's daily activities with the stated mission. Ask team members for their quick reactions. Do the church's activities truly reflect its mission? How specifically might they be adjusted?

29

THE FENCE-POST SYNDROME

Why good leaders go bad

Have you ever wondered why so many good leaders are caught in compromising situations that effectively end their ability to influence others? How did they ever attain positions of responsibility in spite of the character flaws that became apparent after they had risen to the top? Here are three possible explanations.

1. Sometimes insecure people rise to the top of their fields because they overcompensate for a weakness or an unmet emotional need. They eventually succumb to the pressure of the success that this weakness helped motivate. It's a bit like a sinkhole that eventually engulfs everything built on top of it.

2. Other leaders fall because of an unconscious desire to escape the pressures of success. They tire of the constant stress of decision making and the limelight but are too proud or scared to seek help or to step down. They unconsciously sabotage themselves in a plea for help.

3. My favorite explanation is what I call the fence-post syndrome. To build a fence, the builder places posts in the ground then attaches wires to the posts. The posts serve as the foundation. But rain can erode the soil from the base of the post. Eventually, the soil can wash away, leaving the post dangling from the attached wires. Although the post is still a part of the fence, the wires now hold up the post.

Many leaders have built strong, effective churches because of their excellent character. They are admired for their integrity, and people choose to follow them. But success eventually erodes their ethical foundations.

Leaders who begin believing they can do no wrong and trusting their own publicity releases are like fence posts that gradually lose their footings. It rarely happens suddenly. But eventually the church, which was once held up by the leader, begins holding up the leader. This is often not readily apparent from appearances. That is why the Apostle Paul was so adamant in his letters to Timothy that only people of high character should be allowed to lead. Wise leaders understand that humility, accountability, and strong spiritual moorings are essential to avoiding the fence-post syndrome.

LESSON 29

THE FENCE-POST SYNDROME

Why good leaders go bad

Context

Leaders who help build churches can gradually become supported by those churches without realizing it. When they become a weight instead of a support, they threaten the health of the church and its people. Character and moral integrity are vital to a leader's ability to lead and the well-being of the church he or she serves. When leaders fail to uphold high moral standards, they abdicate leadership.

Discussion

1. Identify a time a leader you respected fell. What was the situation, and how did the person reach this point?
2. What is your response to the fence-post syndrome? How can a leader avoid moral and ethical failure?
3. How can boards, policies, and even staff members help leaders avoid character failure, when leaders typically have more power, authority, and influence?
4. What can our church do to provide support and accountability for its leaders?
5. What specifically can you do to avoid pride, poor accountability, and other temptations?

Activity 1

Before this activity, gather a pile of dirt in a large bowl or bucket. As you begin this discussion, slowly pour water onto the top of the dirt so that it erodes. Talk about natural causes of erosion, such as wind, water, and temperature. Then discuss various causes of moral erosion. What tempts people? What special temptations do leaders face? What specific steps can leaders take to guard against those temptations?

Activity 2

Use tape or chalk to outline a 2x2-foot box on the floor. Ask one person to stand on one foot in the box. Push against the person, who will likely lose his or her balance and step out of the box. Ask the person to step back into the box and stand on both feet. Again, push the person to the point that he or she steps out of the box. Discuss the difference between standing on one foot rather than two.

Now recruit someone to stand behind the person. Push the person backward; he or she will probably stay in the box. Try moving the person sideways. If he or she steps out of the box, recruit two more people to stand on each side of the person. Push again. Discuss how the extra stability of standing on two feet and the people surrounding the person kept him or her in the box. Relate this to accountability systems and team support that help prevent leaders from falling.

LESSON

30 FAST TRACKING

Leading at the speed of change

Serious fans of stadium football may scoff at its arena counterpart, but if you've ever watched arena football in person, you know how exciting this fast-paced, high-scoring version of football is. (Now, if those same principles could only be applied to baseball and golf!) Arena football is to twenty-first century leadership what stadium football is to twentieth-century leadership. Change has always been with us, but never at such a rapid speed. As technology, information, and competition proliferate, the need for faster leading increases as well. We used to say that bigger beats up smaller, but now we say that faster eats up slower. You have to change your flat tires without stopping the car. The rate of change will likely not slow down, which means that the gap between those who are willing to change and those who are not will grow.

Adrenaline junkies are addicted to speed for speed's sake, but when speed is necessary to remain productive and relevant during times of rapid change, it is healthy. Many churches, nonprofit organizations, and old-fashioned businesses will sink in this environment unless they change styles and pick up the pace.

Good stewardship demands that we use resources and opportunities properly. Faster leading demands that we multi-task, require fewer approvals, boldly launch new programs, and pull the plug on less effective ones. We cannot afford to leisurely take aim and fire; often we must shoot on the run. Yesterday's leaders may not be able to make the cut. As high school milers are now faster than yesteryear's Olympians, so today's leaders must outpace their predecessors.

Because leading must be faster, we need leaders who are not only bolder and more competent, but also more focused and centered. Blurred vision and instability do not make for better decisions. The demand is greater than ever for leaders who take time to nurture their souls, stay in tune with God, and invest in quiet time. Even in the midst of the frenetic pace of leadership today, wise leaders will take the time to balance their inner and outer worlds.

LESSON 30

FAST TRACKING

Leading at the speed of change

Context

Society and churches are functioning today at speeds that are sometimes overwhelming. Because it is an unchangeable reality, speed must be viewed more as a friend than an enemy. Leaders must not only deal with their own feelings of motion sickness but also coach those who are tempted to put on the brakes.

Discussion

1. List a few ways that life has sped up in the last decade.
2. How do these changes affect you? How have you been forced to respond to them?
3. What is the danger of going too fast?
4. What is the danger of moving too slowly?
5. Name a few things in your area of responsibility that may need to be done more quickly if you are to keep up with change.

Activity 1

Ask one person to stand and hold out his or her hand, palm down, with the "scissor fingers" parted. Dangle a dollar bill between the two spread fingers, and explain that you are going to let go of the bill. Say, "You cannot move your hand up or down, but if you stop the falling bill with your fingers, you can have it." Drop the bill, then repeat the activity several times. (Most people will need several opportunities before they begin to anticipate the drops.) Discuss how slow response to parishioners, a changing community, and competition can cause your church to miss valuable opportunities.

Activity 2

If you have sufficient space, ask the group to participate in any number of relay races such as bouncing a ball down a gym floor, blowing a Ping-Pong ball along the floor from one end of the room to the other, or tossing a water balloon from person to person. Make sure the teams are even, and allow time to practice. Then announce that you will award a prize, such as lunch or early dismissal, to the winning team. After the winning team is declared, discuss why now, more than ever, the fastest churches get the prize. Identify those things your church stands to lose by moving too slowly and what it stands to gain by functioning more quickly.

LESSON

31

WEIGHING IN

Determining people's strengths

One goal of healthy churches is to maximize people's strengths and to minimize their weaknesses, and it is best accomplished by matching people with jobs that take full advantage of their strengths. This goal requires leaders to be excellent judges of their churches' needs as well as the strengths and weaknesses of their people. I have found the following seven ability quotients to be helpful in aligning people's strengths with organizational needs.

1. Intelligence quotient. People with high IQs enjoy complex, conceptual projects, whereas those with low IQs are best suited for concrete, task-oriented roles.

2. People quotient. Folks with high PQs are good with others, excel in customer service, and enjoy highly visible roles. Those with low PQs work best behind the scenes, often at task-oriented jobs.

3. Energy quotient. People with high EQs (rabbits) enjoy having plenty to do. Those with low EQs (turtles) are not necessarily lazy, but they resist being pressured or asked to do more.

4. Resource quotient. People with high RQs generously give their time, talent, or treasure. Those with low RQs may be sincere and dedicated, but they aren't eager to share their personal resources.

5. Attitude quotient. Attitudes are contagious, so put people with highly positive attitudes where they'll influence others. Steer those with negative attitudes away from influential roles.

6. Motivational quotient. Motivation is the engine that drives all the other quotients. People with high MQs are eager to commit to organizational goals, whereas those with low MQs resist. (Leaders are MQ raisers.)

7. Spirituality quotient. It should go without saying that churches must be staffed with folks who have achieved high levels of spiritual maturity. People with high SQs are solid and mature. Those with low SQs often vacillate in their spiritual commitments and become defeated quickly.

Many, if not most, organizational problems arise when people are placed in positions that demand more than their quotients allow. A careful evaluation of both people and expectations is therefore critical to the success of any church.

WEIGHING IN

Determining people's strengths

Context

There are no wrong people, just wrong positions. Leaders are responsible for placing people in positions in which they will excel. When people fail, it's a sign that leadership has failed to accurately assess both the people and the needs of the church.

Discussion

1. Describe an experience in which a leader clearly did not accurately assess the abilities of a team member. What was the outcome?
2. Why is it important to assess a person's strengths *before* recruiting and hiring him or her?
3. What is the greatest challenge in determining the needs of a specific role or task?
4. Why is talent alone not a sufficient indicator of a person's ability to excel in a position?
5. What are some ways to determine a person's strengths when you have limited experience with that person?

Activity 1

In preparation for this activity, gather several children's jigsaw puzzles containing twenty or thirty pieces each. You will need enough puzzles for each team of two to four to have one. Switch a few pieces of some of the puzzles with those of the others. Leave one or two puzzles intact.

Form teams of two to four, give each team a puzzle, and challenge teams to be the first to put their puzzles together. Afterward, relate this experience to the importance of finding people whose strengths fit organizational needs. Discuss how mismatches hinder goal achievement and lead to frustration.

Activity 2

Before this activity, gather inexpensive rings of varying sizes, place each in a bag, and randomly distribute the bags during the meeting. Instruct participants to put the rings on and then stand in a circle to show how the rings fit. Use this funny experience to point out the absurdity of assigning tasks and roles without considering the "sizes" of those who are asked to be responsible for them.

32 PLATE SPINNING

Assessing and responding to priorities

Way back in the '50s and '60s, there was a regular performer on *The Ed Sullivan Show* who used to spin plates on tall sticks. Inevitably, he'd have nearly all the plates spinning when one or two of them would begin to wobble and threaten to fall. He'd run over to the wobbly plates, rotate the sticks a few times, and then try to launch another plate or two. Occasionally plates would fall and crash on the stage.

Leaders today have to be adept plate spinners. But their ability to assess and respond to changing situations and needs has consequences far more important than a few broken plates.

Jesus often reminded his followers of the need to establish priorities. He urged them to "seek first [God's] kingdom" (Matthew 6:33) and to leave their friends and families to follow him (Luke 9:59-62). He told them that investing in things that do not matter is akin to building a house on the sand, where the elements will destroy it (Matthew 7:24-27).

The dictionary defines *triage* as "a system of assigning priorities of medical treatment based on urgency, chance for survival, etc." Doctors using triage give priority to those patients whose wounds and medical conditions are the most urgent and who also have the best chances of survival. So triage sometimes requires doctors to bypass the most severe cases because they stand little chance of surviving. Leaders, too, must often employ the principles of triage in their churches. Expending inordinate energy on matters that have all but died is often poor stewardship.

Here are three ideas for establishing organizational priorities:

1. Ask yourself how far-reaching the problem or opportunity is or could become. You can waste a lot of time attending to minutiae while more significant matters wobble out of control. Attend to things that will have the greatest impact.

2. Ask yourself how the situation could negatively affect morale. For example, the longer personnel issues are allowed to persist, the more difficult they are to fix. Leaders who address potentially negative situations early will save a great deal of effort later.

3. Ask how an oversight in a certain area might cause your church to miss an important opportunity. When should an unspun plate take priority over one that's about to drop? When the potential of the first outweighs that of the second. Leaders often drop valuable plates they've never spun because they're busy investing in plates that matter less.

LESSON 32

PLATE SPINNING

Assessing and responding to priorities

Context

The demand for a leader's attention will almost always outweigh his or her supply of time and energy. That is why it's imperative for leaders to accurately assess and prioritize problems and opportunities.

Discussion

1. Describe an experience in which you ignored a problem or opportunity because you underestimated its importance.

2. List two or three plates that are currently wobbling in your area of responsibility. Which are the most important? On what do you base this assessment?

3. Why is dealing with the urgent not necessarily the best way to prioritize?

4. What can you do to improve your method of encouraging feedback and team input so that your assessments are better informed?

5. What is the biggest challenge you face in keeping your plates spinning?

Activity 1

Before this activity, use masking tape to divide a large open area in half. (If you have access to an indoor gym and volleyball net, even better.) Blow up two or three balloons for each participant.

Ask two people to volunteer to remain neutral during this game, then form two teams of equal size. Ask each team to stand on either side of the dividing line or net. Explain that the goal is to keep all of the balloons in the air without allowing them to touch the floor. Each time a balloon touches the floor, a point will be given to the side it touched. The two neutral participants will count the number of times balloons touch the floor. The team with the fewest points is the winner. Play several one-minute sessions. After a few rounds, discuss the challenges of the game and the strategies the teams developed. Ask them to relate this experience to their real-life prioritization challenges.

Activity 2

Form teams of four or five people each. Give everyone a self-stick note, then ask each person to briefly describe on the note one example of a wobbling plate in the church. Ask team members to randomly place their self-stick notes on a table or wall. Then ask them to work together to prioritize them, assessing the potential damage or loss of each if it's handled inappropriately.

LEADING WITH STYLE

Adopting an appropriate leadership style

Every leader has a certain style of leadership. But to be most effective, leaders must often adapt their styles to fit a variety of situations. Otherwise, they run the risk of seeming to be inappropriate.

Great leaders have demonstrated this ability to adapt their leadership styles to the situations at hand. John 2:13-17 describes Jesus clearing the Temple area with a makeshift whip. This combative style was entirely appropriate to the situation. At other times, he was easygoing and almost detached, asking questions and engaging in thought-provoking conversation.

Here are four leadership styles that a leader may need to adopt as situations warrant.

Commander. When the situation demands fast action or when others don't know what to do or respond lethargically in an urgent situation, a take-charge style is often most appropriate. Although this approach is currently out of favor, there are occasions when it is certainly appropriate for leaders to tell others what to do. In such situations, less assertive methods are usually ineffectual.

Catalyst. When people are fairly motivated and somewhat informed, then a less domineering but still very active leadership style is appropriate. The catalyst actively ensures that team members are motivated and working together and that they understand what needs to be done.

Coach. A coach works from the sidelines to provide instruction and motivation, confronting team members when they aren't performing well or lack motivation. This approach works well when team members are doing a good job. Many professionals and well-educated leaders prefer this kinder, gentler, less hierarchical style of leadership.

Consultant. Motivated, competent people respond well to this relaxed approach to leading. Coming on too strong with people who know what they're doing is a good way to offend and discourage them. The consultant is more of a leader among peers who offers wisdom, helps to create focus, and serves as a team builder.

On any given day, a leader may need to demonstrate all four of these styles as situations change. Churches also change and outgrow certain leadership styles that served them well in the past but are no longer effective. The savvy leader recognizes this and changes leadership styles accordingly.

LESSON 33

LEADING WITH STYLE

Adopting an appropriate leadership style

Context

Most of us have experienced leadership that was inappropriate to the situation either because it was too strong or too weak. To be effective, leaders must accurately assess situations and use appropriate leadership styles to respond to them.

Discussion

1. Discuss an experience in which a leader's style was inappropriate to the situation.
2. What makes reading a situation challenging?
3. Think of one or two situations in which the commander style of leadership would be appropriate. Do the same for the other three styles: catalyst, coach, and consultant.
4. As a leader, which styles do you prefer?
5. How is this preference helpful in accomplishing organizational goals? How could it be unhelpful?

Activity 1

Before this activity, write the following two lists on a white board. Ask the participants to draw lines from the situation to the attire that would be appropriate for each:

dinner on the weekend	suit and tie
funeral or wedding	sweats
working out	business casual
hanging around the house	blue jeans and a T-shirt

Talk about how we consciously choose appropriate attire for the variety of situations we find ourselves in each day. Then relate this to the even more important need to adopt leadership styles that are appropriate to the wide variety of situations we find ourselves in each day.

Activity 2

Read the following scenarios aloud. After each, ask participants to write down the leadership style they recommend and then discuss why they think their responses are correct. The ensuing dialogue will likely reveal other issues to consider when selecting an appropriate style.

SCENARIO 1: *You're the president of a college. The faculty is upset about a new policy that has been recommended by the board of trustees, and you are striving to develop a realistic compromise that will be acceptable to the faculty but will also achieve the goals of the trustees.* (A consultant style would probably be effective in this situation because the participants are highly educated, committed people who want to be involved.)

SCENARIO 2: *Your staff has just coordinated a big event and is in the midst of wrapping up the project. While it was successful, the staff is tired and seems to lack direction.* (A coaching style would probably work well in this situation. The coach would get involved, congratulate the team, and provide guidance for completing the effort.)

SCENARIO 3: *The electricity in your facility has gone out. The computers and other administrative equipment are not functioning. In addition, your church operates a childcare facility on site. The staff is milling around, wondering what to do.* (Adopting the style of a friendly commander would be appropriate in this situation. The urgency of the situation requires a leader who will communicate requests and expectations directly and clearly.)

SCENARIO 4: *People are standing around before a meeting, unsure of what to set up.* (A catalyst would roll up his or her sleeves, find out what needs to be done, and try to give some direction while participating in the solution.)

LEADER HATS

Understanding the emotional needs of followers

There is an emotional side of leading that few leadership books and seminars address. While few team members ever articulate this, they have certain psychological needs that they expect or desire their leaders to fulfill. When these needs aren't met, a leader's influence is reduced.

Great leaders respond in a variety of ways to the people they lead. I call these responses "leader hats," referring to the many roles that a leader plays in the life of a team member, beyond mere organizational necessities.

Parent. A leader often fills the role of a mom and/or dad, even among adults, for people who look for someone who'll provide security, direction, nurturing, counsel, and a sense of community.

Police officer. People in the workplace should be safe from bullies and those who do not play fairly. Leaders must stand up for what is right and create a climate in which bullying is not permitted.

Judge. Establishing policy and making sure that everyone knows and plays by the rules is essential to teamwork. People have confidence in leaders whose judgment calls are fair and balanced.

Counselor. People need leaders who will listen, understand their dilemmas, and provide caring counsel. When leaders appear aloof or uncaring, their influence is diminished.

Pastor. Only those leaders who recognize and understand the moral and spiritual side of humanity are able to provide moral and spiritual support to those they lead. People want their leaders to possess ethical integrity so that they can trust their counsel.

Friend. Sometimes people need to see their leaders let their hair down. There are appropriate times for leaders to laugh, be vulnerable, slap backs, and just be one of the guys or gals. If you never show this side of your personality, those you lead will have a difficult time identifying with you.

Leaders generally assume that their role is primarily to be organizational gurus rather than people who meet the emotional needs of those they lead. Fair or not, people often have unconscious expectations of their leaders that transcend the typical job description. When leaders put on the wrong hat or overlook a person's need, their effectiveness is diluted. While leaders can't be all things to all people, savvy leaders are aware of the emotional needs of those they lead and respond appropriately.

LESSON 34

LEADER HATS

Understanding the emotional needs of followers

Context

Leading just got more complicated. When you think about the unconscious and emotional needs of the people you lead, you begin to realize why the job of leading can be so difficult. Leaders who fail to recognize these needs tend to have less influence and are often frustrated because they don't understand why.

Discussion

1. What do you think of the concept of "leader hats"?
2. Can you think of an instance in which a leader failed to recognize or respond to the unconscious needs of the people he or she served? What was the result?
3. Why do you think so few leadership books or workshops address this topic?
4. What are other examples of leader hats?
5. What factors make it difficult for leaders to wear the right hats?

Activity 1

Before this activity, gather a variety of hats. Ask participants to close their eyes as you place a hat on each person's head. Tell them that, without touching their hats, they may each ask the other participants up to five questions in an attempt to identify who might wear their hats. After five questions, each person will guess what kind of hat he or she is wearing and then remove it.

Relate this experience to the demand for leaders to wear different hats to respond to the emotional needs of those they lead.

Activity 2

Read the following scenarios aloud. After each, ask participants to identify which "hat" would be appropriate for a leader to wear in responding to it. (Often several hats should be worn at once; these scenarios are presented to spark discussion.)

• *Bill continually exceeds his departmental budget but apparently doesn't consider it cause for concern, while other team members are doing their best to stay within budget.* (A leader would have to wear the hat of the police officer in this situation and encourage Bill to play by the rules.)

• *Two or three team members are perturbed by another and begin saying negative things about her.* (The parent's hat may be appropriate in this situation, as the staff needs to be told to find positive ways to get along.)

• *A team member tells you about his marital problems and his worries about his children.* (The counselor's hat is called for as the leader provides a listening ear and support.)

• *A staff member confides that he feels his life is going nowhere. He's been drinking a bit too much and is not sure what to do.* (The role of pastor is required in this situation. The pastor would encourage the staff member to talk more about his feelings and would offer to pray for him.)

• *Staff members are sitting around, shooting the breeze. They are laughing about something funny that happened to one of them.* (A leader who dons the hat of a friend would stop what he or she is doing and participate.)

• *A team member consistently arrives late for work and leaves early. The leader also suspects that this person's phone calls are dominated by personal chat.* (A leader wearing a judge's hat would remind the employee of established policy and ensure that it's upheld.)

RECIPE FOR CHANGE

The four transitioning ingredients

Change. Effective leaders recognize the need for it and are able to lead a church through it. They know that change for change's sake is irresponsible and potentially disastrous. What they really aim for is improvement. So why does the very idea of change cause such distress? The biggest reason is that transitions into change are mishandled. Before implementing a change, a consideration of the following four factors will help you determine how well the change will be received and implemented.

1. Readiness. First ask yourself how ripe your people are for the improvement. People are unwilling to accept a solution to a problem they don't perceive. Sometimes people won't be open to change until their discomfort is very great, but unfortunately, this often occurs too late in the game. Thus, leaders must teach, communicate, cast vision, and even help create discomfort as part of a transition into necessary change.

2. Leadership strength. The more people trust a leader, the faster a new idea will take root in a church. Natural leaders often intuitively sense when it is right to make changes. When faith in a leader is not so strong, more time and preparation will be necessary before change can be successfully implemented.

3. Time. People need time to process change. The faster you go, the more difficult the transition process is likely to be. Be sure to invest sufficient time to plan, communicate, and process new ideas. Depending upon the magnitude of the change, it may take up to five years to implement.

4. Impact. Ask yourself how much the innovation will affect the church. Minor changes will create far less stress than larger ones. If a big change is required, be sure to invest in the necessary preparation.

Considering these four factors will help you focus on improving transitions from the status quo. Change tends to be logical, left-brained, and strategic. Transitions tend to be emotional, right-brained, and relational. Transitions are more difficult than changes. By underestimating the former, we reduce the potential of the latter.

LESSON 35

RECIPE FOR CHANGE

The four transitioning ingredients

Context

Changes are often not as painful as the transitions leading into them. How leaders adopt innovations is often as important as the innovations themselves. Leaders who are oblivious to the differences between improvement plans and transition plans are almost guaranteed to have more problems in implementing change. Instead of blaming those who thwart change, savvy leaders take responsibility for creating processes that allow new ideas to be nurtured.

Discussion

1. Can you recall a change that was poorly received and implemented? As you consider the four transition factors (readiness, leadership strength, time, and impact), what do you think went wrong?
2. Why is readiness an important factor in change?
3. Why is leadership strength an important factor in change?
4. Why is time an important factor in change?
5. Why is impact an important factor in change?

Activity 1

Before this activity, find a road map that includes the area around your city or town. Choose a desti-nation that can be reached from your city or town by several possible routes, and plot an indirect, out-of-the-way path. Make enough copies to give one to each team of two to four people.

Ask people to form teams, distribute the maps, and instruct teams to find new ways to reach the destination. When they've finished, ask them to report their findings to the other teams. Discuss how this exercise illustrates the need to consider other ways of doing what you do in your church.

Add a twist to this exercise by changing the destination after teams have mapped out their routes. For example, you might say, "What if you want to get to Chicago instead of Kansas City? How would the new destination affect your plan?" This question addresses the possibility that the goal, as well as the method of achieving it, may have to change.

Activity 2

Ask participants to identify one change that is being contemplated for your church. Ask them to rate the four transition factors according to the scale below.

Rate the team's or congregation's readiness on this scale: 1—will fight the idea; 2—will passively resist; 3—will be neutral; 4—will be receptive; 5—will promote the idea.

Rate the leader on this scale: 1—little influence; 2—some influence; 3—moderate influence; 4—strong influence; 5—very strong influence.

Rate the time on this scale: 1—up to six months; 2—six months to a year; 3—one to two years; 4—two to three years; 5—three to five years.

Rate the impact on this scale: 1—trivial; 2—small; 3—medium; 4—large; 5—enormous.

Now use the following formula to estimate the effect the transition will have on your church.

(readiness ____ + leader strength _____) x time _____ ÷ impact _____ = _____ transition factor

Transition Factors: 0.4-1.5—dangerous; 1.6-2.9—be careful; 3.0-4.9—positive; 5-20—optimum; 21-50—overly ripe (you've waited too long).

If the transition factor is less than optimal, what can you do to change the various factors to achieve a better transition? You may find that this activity leads to a follow-up meeting to address this question. For more information, see *How to Change Your Church (Without Killing It)* by Alan E. Nelson and Gene Appel, Word Publishing, 2000.

LESSON **36**

TIME'S UP

Knowing when to step down

K nowing when to step down from a position of leadership is more an art than a science. Unforced exits require Solomon-like wisdom. The tendency among most leaders is to quit too soon. The "greener grass" syndrome, weariness, and the need to see tangible progress are all very real factors that tempt leaders to pull up roots too quickly. Every farmer knows that it takes time to grow a crop. The harvest doesn't happen the day after planting. As organizational farmers, some leaders crave instant success. Delayed gratification is as great a challenge for leaders as anyone else, but the stakes are much higher for leaders. People depend upon leaders to be resilient over the long haul. They need to trust their leaders to be willing to persevere, to endure, and to stay committed for the distance. Giving up is a common and frequent yearning among leaders. Daydream if you must, and temporarily escape the pressures of leadership as needed via movies, hobbies, and vacations, but don't let the grind of the journey prevent you from fulfilling your calling.

While many leaders leave too soon, others stay too long. Sometimes leaders listen too intently to those around them rather than concentrating on honest soul-searching to make a decision about whether to stay or leave. Here are three good questions to consider carefully.

1. Has another opportunity arisen that will significantly expand your potential? Making a lateral move, starting over, and even making a modest move upward may not justify leaving your current position. Every career change carries risks. Disdain for the familiar can distort your estimate of a new opportunity's potential. Unless there is a significant chance for you to use your gifts more effectively, remain committed. Never assume that change for change's sake is the right solution.

2. Have you outlived your effectiveness? Your primary goal is to help the church, not yourself, succeed. Waiting for retirement or for just the right new opportunity to come along is a weak reason to endure. You exist to make the church better, not vice versa. Good leaders look for cues around them to know if they've maximized their effectiveness. Have you tried all your viable ideas? Do the folks around you think your time is up? Are others coming up with better ideas and demonstrating greater passion and more focused vision?

3. Have you prepared for your departure? Is a successor in place? Are your files, staff, and other helpful resources in order? Have you given sufficient time to make the transition smooth, or are you leaving suddenly? Are there barriers you can remove to make your successor's job easier? Are you ready to go

LESSON **36**   TIME'S UP

with grace, thanking those who've been good team members, blessing good memories, and remaining silent toward enemies and detractors?

Seeking God's wisdom, relying on your own experience, and seeking the honest counsel of those you trust are all essential when deciding when to move on. Above all, remember that a good leader always puts the welfare of the church ahead of his or her own.

LESSON

TIME'S UP

Knowing when to step down

Context

Birthing is usually easier than dying; arriving is often easier than leaving. Leaders need to understand when it is proper for them to move on so that the church and those depending upon it may thrive.

Discussion

1. Can you think of an example of a leader who left too soon? What happened? What were some of the negative results?

2. Can you think of a leader who stayed too long? What signals did the leader miss? Why do you think he or she stayed too long?

3. Can you think of a leader who left at the right time and did so properly? What made the exit so effective?

4. What signs would you look for in your church that would tell you it's time to leave?

5. How do you determine when it is best to persevere and when it is best to resign? What specific indicators can you rely on in making this distinction?

Activity 1

Before this activity, gather three bananas, each in a different stage of ripeness: green, firm but ripe, and soft and overly ripe.

Ask for a volunteer, then blindfold him or her. One at a time, place a chunk of each banana in the volunteer's mouth. After he or she has tasted all three bananas, ask him or her to describe the differences in terms of taste and texture. Relate this experience to leaders who leave too early, too late, and at just the right time. Ask participants to share something they've learned about leaving well.

Activity 2

This is a fun modification of a relay race. Ask participants to remove their shoes. Pile all the shoes at the opposite end of a large room, gym, or outdoor area. Form two teams, and ask them to line up for a relay race. Explain that each person must run to the pile of shoes, put on any single shoe that is *not* his or her own, and then run back. In order to count, the shoe must be worn all the way from the pile to the starting point. After all the shoes are gone, the team that has recovered the most shoes wins.

After the laughter, discuss what happens when leaders outgrow their roles and need to find a better fit. Also discuss what happens when leaders are unable to fill their positions and are in over their heads.

37

LEADING UP

How to influence peers and those with authority over you

Have you ever driven a car with passengers who influenced you to speed up, slow down, turn here or there, or pull into a favorite fast-food joint? We refer to these people as back-seat drivers. Although the person behind the wheel has the power to direct the car, the driver can be influenced to do things he or she would not do otherwise.

Leaders should be aware that their influence extends beyond those they serve. This range of influence means that they need to consider how to lead laterally; they need to understand how to lead the people who are their peers, share their resources, or hold similar positions of authority and responsibility. They also need to think about how to influence those who have authority over them: their bosses.

Understanding how to influence those over you is akin to knowing how to drive from the back seat. While you may not have the steering wheel in your hands, you can certainly influence where the vehicle goes. Influencing the driver requires that you understand what makes him or her tick. Here are five questions to ask yourself as you seek to influence the influencers.

1. What are their burdens, passions, and concerns? Understand what consumes a leader's mind. Learn how he or she desires to be communicated with, handles stress, and relates to people. Strive more to understand than to be understood.

2. Who are their gatekeepers? While you might not know the influencer, you may know someone who does. It's helpful to know secretaries, assistants, family members, and friends of influencers.

3. How can you help them succeed? Don't think only of what you want from the leader; consider also how you can help him or her reach goals. Look for the win/win.

4. What is the best timing? You will set yourself up for failure if you ask a favor when your leader is drained or you seek time when he or she is fully committed elsewhere. Do your homework. Know the best times and situations in which to approach a leader.

5. How do you keep in touch? Notes, e-mails, and phone messages are good ways to build and maintain a relationship. Stay in touch with your leader so that, when you need to cross the relationship bridge, you can.

Some may consider these tools political manipulation, but really they're little more than smart people skills. Leading involves power. If you want to lead more effectively, you need to know who has power and how they can share it. With the overall good in mind, you can serve best when you know how to "lead up."

LESSON 37

LEADING UP

*How to influence peers and
those with authority over you*

Context

When people with influence do not know you or your concerns, they may unintentionally thwart your goals. Tapping into the influence resources of others is a strategic way to bring power to your leadership and get things done.

Discussion

1. Describe a situation in which you were prevented from achieving a goal because someone with more power limited your ability.
2. Why do you think it's important to lead laterally and up, as well as down?
3. List the names of those who should be on your "up" list—people you should get to know and improve your ability to influence.
4. What are their concerns and personalities? Who are their gatekeepers? What are possible contact points?
5. What is something you want to achieve for those you lead, and who is an influencer who can help you so that you both win?

Activity 1

Before the activity, arrange to have cars available for all the participants to drive or ride in. Privately give two sets of instructions. Tell the drivers to take a short, direct route to a specific destination unless they're persuaded to do otherwise. Tell the passengers to try to persuade their drivers to deviate from their route to do something the drivers would prefer to do. Tell everyone to report back in fifteen minutes. When they do, discuss what happened and relate back seat driving to leading up and leading laterally.

Activity 2

Play the children's game Red Light, Green Light to illustrate some of the principles of this lesson. Designate one person to stand twenty or thirty feet from a starting line, and have everyone else stand behind the starting line. Remind participants of the rules of the game: The designated person will turn his or her back to the players and shout, "Green light!" The runners will take as many steps toward the finish line as possible before the designated person shouts, "Red light!" and turns around to face the runners. Anyone who is caught moving must return to the starting line and begin again. The first person to cross the finish line wins.

Afterward, discuss the game. How did the designated person diminish hopes of accomplishment? What were some ways to move forward, and how were participants set back? How do these experiences relate to leadership?

GATEKEEPERS

Getting through to those who influence the influencers

In medieval times, castles were often surrounded by walls and moats. To provide entrance to the castle, a gatekeeper would lower a drawbridge over the moat. The gatekeeper prevented beggars and enemies of the feudal lord or king from entering and would be punished if he betrayed that trust. Anyone wanting to enter the castle was helped by an alliance with the gatekeeper.

In some ways society has changed little from medieval times. While the gate-keeping function is now informal and unofficial, it is still important. Leaders still entrust to others the task of barring entry to those who would waste their time and resources. Gatekeepers still allow or deny access to people in positions of power.

The story of Queen Esther illustrates the idea that often *who* you know is just as important as *what* you know. Even though Esther's cousin, who learned of a plan to annihilate the Jews, didn't have direct access to the powerful king, he knew that the queen did. Because she could get the king's ear, she was able to deliver her cousin's message and prevent her people from being annihilated.

Who are the gatekeepers in your professional life? No matter who you are, you can only know and be surrounded by a small group of people. Therefore, whether you are the President of the United States or a PTA chairperson, certain people have greater access to you than others. Formal gatekeepers include sec-retaries, assistants, superiors, and subordinates. Informal gatekeepers are family members, friends, and network contacts. "Do you know anyone who knows _____?" is a common question among leaders, because they seek people who can help them contact other influential people.

While some may view this as politics and gamesmanship, it is simply rela-tionship building. By getting to know and winning the trust of someone who has gained the trust of another, you can communicate with and gain access to people of influence. When you avoid this sort of relationship building, you diminish your leadership and ultimately let down those you serve.

When you insult an administrative assistant or snub someone because he or she is not a person of prominence, you may have just hamstrung your ability to get to know the more powerful person. Ignoring the "little people" usually comes back to haunt you. People who know who the gatekeepers are and invest in building relationships with them are far more likely to gain access to power holders. Power is a vital leadership resource; you can't get much done without it. Therefore, identify the gatekeepers, develop relationships with them, and at the appropriate time, you can ask them to lower the drawbridge.

LESSON 38

GATEKEEPERS

Getting through to those who influence the influencers

Context

Leadership is not just about knowing your team and other leaders. You also need to know those who influence the influencers.

Discussion

1. Identify one person you've gotten to know through a gatekeeper.
2. Think of one person who has gotten to know you through one of your gatekeepers.
3. List two or three people who could help you accomplish some of your organizational goals.
4. List two or three gatekeepers for each of these people.
5. Can you think of a time a gatekeeper prevented you from meeting someone? What did you learn from this?

Activity 1

Before this activity, arrange to have access to a room that can be locked with a key. (If this isn't possible, adapt the activity to work with a lockbox.) Gather a variety of keys, enough for each participant to choose one. Be sure that one of the keys will unlock the door to the meeting room. Place something good to eat, such as cookies, in the room and lock it. Put all the keys in a box.

Ask everyone to choose a key, and inform participants that something very good to eat is behind the locked door. Participants must first find out who has the correct key then persuade that person to let them in. Afterward, discuss the importance of identifying the person with the right key, the process of persuading him or her, and the benefits of the key to the one who held it.

Activity 2

Ask participants to quickly brainstorm a list of favors that might be available to them on the basis of their connections. Ask them what they can obtain—that another person in the group probably can't get as easily—by calling one of their contacts. For example, the favor might be a few minutes to talk to someone who is well-known or busy or a reservation on short notice at a popular restaurant.

Discuss the importance to effective leadership of knowing gatekeepers, networking, and constantly making new contacts.

LEADING BEAUTIFULLY

The importance of timeliness

"He has made everything beautiful in its time" (Ecclesiastes 3:11). King Solomon's words reflect the cycles of living organisms. Churches are also alive. At times they are served best by management and maintenance. At other times they must be changed and renewed. Starting, ending, selling, servicing, hiring, firing, training, team building, confronting, budgeting, fundraising—all are beautiful in their time, but the right thing at the wrong time is...ugly. It's often as bad as the wrong thing and occasionally can be worse. (Of course, there is no right time for the wrong thing.)

The best time for a child to share a less-than-desirable report card is not right after his or her parent arrives home after a long day at work. The child would be better off to wait until the parent is well rested and cheerful. When the stock market is low, it's a good time to buy. When it's high, it may be a good time to sell. In baseball, batters strike out when they incorrectly assess the timing of the pitch. What is true of individuals is also true of churches.

Typical leadership books discuss the *what* and the *how* of various organizational functions, but most do not address the finer art of *when*. Determining the proper time to initiate change is one of leadership's greatest challenges. Good leaders know that many wonderful solutions will yield minimal results if the timing is off.

The ancient Greek culture had two words for time: *chronos* and *kairos*. The former has to do with measuring time; it conveys quantity. The latter has to do with appropriateness; it conveys quality—rightness and ripeness. In our culture, we're used to *chronos*; we think of time in terms of how long something will take and at what point on the calendar something will begin. A more Eastern mindset considers the quality of time by asking when a decision is right. Waiting for the right time should not be confused with passivity. Leaders can use their influence to hasten the ripening process.

Shrewd leaders must constantly ask, "Is this the right time for this decision?" Those who make sweeping changes when the time is ripe for managing and maintaining won't see beautiful results. Even though their motives may be good, impatient leaders often do a disservice to those they lead. It's also dangerous to wait too long to implement a new change because an opportunity may be lost. Being in touch with both the church and the environment is essential in determining appropriate timing. It's a beautiful thing when leaders do the right thing at the right time.

LESSON 39

LEADING BEAUTIFULLY

The importance of timeliness

Context

Leaders are sometimes perplexed when necessary organizational activities yield few results. This lack of effectiveness is often not because what they've done is wrong; it's because something else was needed more at that time.

Discussion

1. Can you think of an example of a leader doing the right thing at the wrong time? What were the results?
2. How can you know the right time for a specific organizational task or emphasis?
3. What can you do to ripen conditions for change?
4. Think of an example in your leadership experience when you emphasized *chronos* to the detriment of *kairos*.
5. Which do you think is the most common timing error—initiating change too early or too late?

Activity 1

Before the meeting, bake three small cakes (or enlist the help of someone who will do this for you). Remove one from the oven at the appropriate time, according to the recipe. Remove another significantly early and the third significantly late.

Ask team members to sample each cake. Discuss the differences in taste, then explain the causes. Finally, discuss the importance of timing in your church.

Activity 2

Before this activity, gather a variety of caps and hats in a lot of sizes. Distribute them to participants and ask them to try the hats on without adjusting the size. Ask, "Is this hat a good fit?" Record the number of people who say yes. Then instruct them to pass the hat to someone else. Again, ask if the hats fit, and record the feedback. Do this a few more times. Talk about how some hats fit certain people better than others. Relate this to how certain organizational activities may fit certain occasions and not fit others. Just as one size doesn't fit all, one time doesn't fit all.

LESSON 40

SOCIAL BANKING

Knowing how much influence you can draw upon

"There are no free lunches." Everything seems to cost something, even if the cost isn't measured in money. This is also true in leadership, where exchanging favors, rewards, tasks, resources, talent, and time contribute to organizational achievement. Leaders must think of themselves as social bankers, people who encourage others to invest in the leadership process. But before people will invest in them, leaders must make deposits in the emotional accounts of those they lead.

When people are somehow enriched through their involvement in a church; when they feel fulfilled; when they find meaning by using their gifts, developing friendships, or earning their leaders' esteem, they place invisible but very real commitment deposits in their leaders' influence accounts. But leading costs. Leaders have to ask for favors, make demands of time and energy, and set challenging goals, all of which depletes their social bank accounts. Leaders can consistently make withdrawals only if they are also generating deposits.

Good leaders continually check their social bank balances. Affirmation cards, thank you notes, recognition of personal achievements, and community building are all ways of increasing the balance in a leader's social account. On the other hand, when leaders request or require more than they deposit, they will eventually overdraw and, at that point, lose their ability to influence others. People will either close out their accounts and leave, or they'll wait until there is a sufficient positive balance before allowing withdrawals.

Effective leaders are good at accruing sufficient emotional deposits. They know their current balance and estimate the cost of the goal or task at hand. They realize that they can push their people only so far without replenishing their relationships in a variety of ways. On the other hand, effective leaders also know not to waste sizable social bank accounts by hoarding them. Their job is to wisely invest the balance in order to benefit the church and the people it serves. Jesus' parable of the wise steward condemns the person who "hid his talent" and did not use it to make a profit. Leaders are not in a popularity contest to earn respect for themselves. They are in the business of raising social capital in order to achieve significant goals on behalf of the church and people they serve.

Effective leaders know that they don't have unlimited influence because of their reputation, position, or past successes. They are social bankers who are sensitive to where they stand at any given time. They look for cues among those they trust, people who know the church and are in touch with other decision-makers and influencers. So whether or not you think of yourself a banker, you are if you want to lead.

LESSON 40

SOCIAL BANKING

*Knowing how much influence
you can draw upon*

Context

When leaders fail to understand the principle of social banking, they underestimate the importance of gaining emotional commitment and tend to overspend the emotional capital of those they lead. Unabated, this habit eventually bankrupts the leader's influence and severely limits organizational achievement.

Discussion

1. Think of a situation in which a leader overestimated his or her social bank account. What happened?
2. What are some practical ways to accurately gauge the balance of your social account as a leader?
3. What are some practical ways to increase your balance?
4. What are some goals or demands in your area of responsibility that will drain your account?
5. How does your estimate of your balance affect how fast you go, how much you expect, and what you do to improve your balance?

Activity 1

Before this activity, gather a variety of items, such as gum, candy bars, mints, cups of coffee, doughnuts, and fruit, and attach a price tag to each. Display the items on a table.

Form groups of five to eight, and distribute varying amounts of Monopoly money to each person. Make sure that the amounts aren't the same.

Go around the circle of participants, allowing each person to buy, trade, or pass—one transaction per turn. After everyone has had three or four turns, discuss the results. Then turn the discussion toward social influence, examining how social capital can be overdrawn and how leaders with bigger balances can accomplish more.

Activity 2

Give everyone a stack of self-stick notes. Ask participants to work as individuals or in teams to identify ways that leaders add deposits to their social bank accounts and ways they withdraw from them. Ask them to write each idea on a self-stick note. Then place each note on a wall or white board under an "asset" or "debt" column.

Examples of assets are credibility, personal affirmations, favors, time, expertise, inclusion, competence, a good track record, personal attention, trust, good communication, logic, accomplishments, and shared rewards.

Examples of debts are insults, mistrust, poor communication, failure, inaction, inability to confront well, ingratitude, blaming, anger, incompetence, fear, lack of vision, pushing too hard with few results, and asking for too much too fast.

Discuss how leaders create positive or negative net worth in terms of their influence. Why do some continue to build credit while others go bankrupt?

HUMBLE PIE

Becoming a true servant-leader

In *Spirituality and Leadership* (NavPress, 2002), I discuss some of the ways that leadership can endanger the soul. One danger is power. While power is necessary for effective leadership, it can be toxic to one's character and spirituality.

Another danger is egotism. Leaders tend to be upfront, go-to people for permission granting, problem solving, and advice giving. They are better known than others. All of this tends to inflate their egos. Fame, influence, position, and perks can easily lead to excessive pride, arrogance, and conceit.

A true leader recognizes that leading is neither more nor less than serving. Humility is not the opposite of power, healthy pride, and self-esteem. In fact, it engenders strong, confident, effective leading. Humble leaders recognize that their job is to serve others with their gifts so that their followers, in turn, may maximize their own gifts and talents.

Common leaders think of themselves as people who seize opportunities and help others and organizations get things done. Some see themselves as leaders who serve. But uncommon leaders think of themselves as servants...who lead.

Just as waiters use menus and trays to serve and teachers use textbooks and knowledge to serve and trash haulers use containers and trucks to serve, servant-leaders use the tools of their trade to benefit others. These tools—position and the ability to influence—are the towel and basin for washing others' feet. While a common leader has servants who wash his or her feet, the servant-leader washes the feet of those he or she serves.

After you've been in the company of a servant-leader, you feel *more* impressed with yourself, not less. You don't feel intimidated; you feel motivated. You are enthusiastic about participating, and you desire to commit. Trust, a staple in leadership, grows faster with a servant-leader. You don't question a servant-leader's motives, and you don't feel manipulated. After leaving the presence of a servant-leader, you want to be like him or her, someone who is humble yet confident, peaceful yet passionate. Servant-leaders are not necessarily less vocal or energetic, weaker, or more persuadable. But they do exude humility in all they do. They are not really concerned with who gets the credit. They rarely sacrifice relationships for outcomes. Yet they produce. Because they bring out the best in people, they achieve more over the long haul.

Jesus washed his disciples' feet and then told them, "You should do as I have done for you." (John 13:15). Your leadership is a reflection of your character. The twenty-first century is hungry for strong, tenacious servant-leaders who put others before themselves and practice what they preach as servants.

OK TO COPY

LESSON 41

HUMBLE PIE

Becoming a true servant–leader

Context

Whether you work in the church or in business, the world is hungry for leaders who are humble and service-minded. The challenge for leaders is that power and humility don't often go hand in hand. Maintaining both requires strong moral fiber, accountability, and conscious effort.

Discussion

1. Describe a servant-leader you've met. What made this person an attractive leader?
2. Why are power and humility difficult to balance?
3. What distinguishes a servant who leads from a leader who serves?
4. Why is it important not to confuse a humble servant with someone who has the capacity to be a servant-leader?
5. What can you do to foster a servant's attitude as you lead?

Activity 1

Use this activity to help participants grasp the differences between a true servant-leader and a traditional leader. Give everyone a stack of self-stick notes. Ask participants to write a characteristic, trait, or adjective that describes leaders on each note. After the group has come up with twenty to fifty different descriptors, stick the notes on a wall or white board. Then ask the group to decide whether each should be placed under the heading "leader" or "servant-leader." Some traits will apply to both headings, and some will clearly apply to only one. Ask participants to explain their choices.

Activity 2

A powerful way to illustrate servant-leadership is to conduct a foot-washing ceremony. Depending on your situation, you may want to wash the feet of all your staff members or the feet of just one person on your staff. Or you may choose to invite spouses, children, or congregants to take part in this session. Participants will be humbled and touched by this act of service, as you model Jesus' humility. You and they will gain a deeper understanding of what it means to serve and lead at the same time.

LESSON 42

TEAM BURS

Removing the things that bug team members

Horsemen know that a small bur between a horse and its saddle will eventually become an irritant that diverts the animal's attention from obeying the rider. That's why riders are careful to remove burs from under their saddles. Bur removal is also the job of a leader. Team members can easily lose their concentration and become less effective because their attention is diverted by rather small matters. Here is a brief list of some of the common burs that bug team members.

Work conditions. Adequate workspace and lighting, comfortable air temperature, and appropriate sound levels are vital to basic human functioning. Sometimes seemingly minor matters in the environment can interrupt normal work and lower productivity.

Communication. When workers rarely hear from "the boss" or when that communication is fuzzy, they tend to fill in the blanks. When this happens, the temptation is toward negative rather than positive interpretation of events. Clear, frequent communication fosters security and confidence among those you serve.

Unclear goals. When goals are vague, people waste a lot of time and energy, often with little to show for it. Meandering is a common organizational problem that clear objectives will help to minimize.

Inadequate resources. Asking people to accomplish goals without giving them adequate materials and tools frustrates and discourages them and is counterproductive. Adequate support staff, equipment, and budget resources are necessary for the long-term health and productivity of a church and its staff.

Irritating team members. Dysfunctional team members can substantially reduce their teams' effectiveness and lower their morale. Listen and look for hints, because other team members may not confront you or the person causing the trouble.

Unfair rewards. When rewards are sporadic, haphazard, and subjective, it is easy for team members to become resentful. Working hard with limited applause, recognition, and remuneration leads to discouragement and a lack of motivation.

Nonsensical rules. Churches need rules, but when the rules seem unfair or arbitrary, complaints will distract workers from the tasks at hand. It is the leader's job to periodically review all policies to make sure they're still relevant.

The Bible refers to leaders as shepherds. Psalm 23 describes the good shepherd, who gently cares for the well-being of the flock. This model is a good one for twenty-first century leaders, who must be aware of the small things that can cause big frustrations among those they serve.

LESSON 42

TEAM BURS

Removing the things that bug team members

Context

Distractions at work may be as simple and as aggravating as flies at a picnic or mosquitoes at a camp-out. The leader's job is to remove the annoyances and irritants that distract people from their responsibilities.

Discussion

1. What common distractions have you experienced that have kept you from concentrating on your work?

2. What are three or four burs that should be removed from our church?

3. How can you gather better feedback from team members to ensure that you're aware of the things that are irritating them and distracting them from their work?

4. Can you think of a bur that was ignored and allowed to become a bigger deal than it should have been?

5. What if you can't or choose not to remove a hindrance to team effectiveness (such as a bothersome teammate, an insufficient budget, or crummy office space)? How do you differentiate between legitimate concerns and trivial complaints?

Activity 1

Place a number of tiny stones (one-eighth to one-quarter inch in diameter) on a table. Ask participants to remove their shoes, put two or three stones in each shoe, and put their shoes on again. Have everyone walk around the room one time while reciting the Pledge of Allegiance, the Lord's Prayer, or something else they've memorized. Afterward, relate the stones to the minor irritants that distract people from the tasks at hand.

Activity 2

Make a skillet of scrambled eggs. "Accidentally" scramble some eggshells with the eggs. Pass out samples for participants to eat, and watch their reactions. Discuss how the shells, which were minor parts of the whole and not detrimental in and of themselves, ruined participants' enjoyment of the food. Equate presence of the eggshells to the minor issues that distract folks from their work.

LONELY AT THE TOP

Dealing with the unique emotions of a leader

Whether the cause is staffing problems, discouragement, the pressure of finances, an overcommitted schedule, or a crisis in the community, leading can be a heavy burden. A big difference between leaders and those they serve is that it's inadvisable for the former to express negative emotions to the latter. As a result, most battles are played out quietly in leaders' minds, causing them to feel alone.

Some may advise leaders not to pretend to be stronger than they are, to be real, let go, and tell it like it is. After all, leaders are only human. This advice is unwise because leaders *aren't* just like everyone else—they have influence. Their emotions have a greater impact on others. They can do a great injustice to those they serve by indiscriminately expressing their disappointment, fear, and apprehension. Leaders must constantly weigh their words, evaluating what to say, how much to say, and to whom. Confiding their discouragement to those they serve will usually diminish their ability to lead.

Leaders throughout history have experienced feelings of aloneness and isolation. Psalms is full of prayers expressing discouragement, fear, and anger. Many are King David's feelings and thoughts as he bore the burden of leading the nation of Israel. At times, only God can fully understand the weighty burdens that leaders carry. God is not intimidated by our anger, and he can give us courage when we're afraid. He will not think less of us for our honesty. Prayer is the best spiritual and psychological therapy for any leader.

At the end of a long day, a grinding week, or a discouraging setback, hang on. Part of your job is to keep hope alive among those you serve, and that hope begins with you. Many are depending on you to demonstrate faith. Seek the advice of trusted friends outside your church. Enjoy the comfort of family and friends. Read and contemplate, but most of all, take time to unload on God.

OK TO COPY

LESSON 43

LONELY AT THE TOP

Dealing with the unique emotions of a leader

Context

A leader should never assume that, just because other leaders don't openly share feelings of discouragement and frustration, they don't have those feelings. People often compare their insides with others' outsides and feel less capable as a result. Rest assured; all leaders sometimes feel discouraged and alone. It helps to know that discouragement and loneliness are normal, but the greatest help comes from confiding in God through prayer.

Discussion

1. What do you think is the loneliest part of leading?
2. What are the dangers of sharing your feelings of fear, discouragement, and anxiety with team members?
3. Why do you think leaders do not more commonly share their frustrations with other leaders who might understand their plights?
4. What is a hurt you experienced as a leader that you couldn't share at the time?
5. Why do you think other people have a difficult time understanding leaders' burdens?

Activity 1

Create an atmosphere of contemplation and reflection by dimming the lights and playing soft music. Distribute paper, and ask participants to journal challenges they are currently facing in their leadership. After about ten minutes, encourage participants to turn these burdens over to God.

Activity 2

Tell participants that most leaders need encouragement, even if they don't act like it. Ask them each to write down the names of three or four leaders they know. Then encourage them to write, call, or e-mail these leaders, letting them know they're thinking of them and want to encourage them in their leading. Encourage participants to express their appreciation for these people and to include them in their prayers.

44

HEAD SLAVE

Modeling servant leadership

In his classic book *Leadership Is an Art*, Max DePree says the "first responsibility of a leader is to define reality. The last is to say thank you." The best leaders—servant-leaders—express their gratitude consistently and sincerely to those they serve. An attitude of gratitude is one of the most important qualities leaders can offer. It fosters teamwork and harnesses the commitment and indebtedness of those they serve.

People loathe being used. They hate the idea that they merely fill a position and are just one more cog in an organization. They want to make a difference, and they long to be appreciated. Servant-leaders exist to help others succeed, and they convey this message consistently and often. This is easier said than done, because the natural inclination is to think others owe the leaders for their jobs, their roles, and their salaries. The challenge for the leader, then, is twofold: first to develop an attitude of gratitude and then to find meaningful ways to manifest it.

To express thanks, use notes, e-mails, and cards to say, "You're doing a great job!" "Keep up the good work!" and "We couldn't do it without you." Verbalize your appreciation often and be specific. Don't just say, "Good job." Instead, say, for example, "You did a wonderful job on the last newsletter. The graphics are super, and the layout is neat and crisp." Whether the staff is paid to do these things is not the point. It's always important to show your appreciation of paid and unpaid team members alike. One of a leader's greatest responsibilities is to make those who serve with him or her feel esteemed.

Occasionally ask your leaders what you can do for them. Intentionally come early to set up and stay late to clean up. Serve coffee, and find ways to show that no job is menial if it needs to be done. Obviously, you can't invest a great deal of your time in these tasks, or you'll be accused of not doing your job, which is leading. But never talk down to people whose roles seem less important than yours. Your job is to nurture a culture of service, and you can't do this without practicing what you preach.

Jesus said that if you want to lead, you must learn to serve. When you are secure in your identity, you are able to wash feet. When you are insecure, you will avoid such tasks. Hold your immediate team members accountable for modeling servanthood as well. Imagine what life would be like if your entire church caught the spirit of humility and everyone served each other. It might just be heaven.

OK TO COPY

LESSON 44

HEAD SLAVE

Modeling servant leadership

ways to model a true servant's heart is to do a kind deed anonymously. Ask participants each to spend five minutes thinking of and writing down one thing they will do within the next week to serve someone anonymously. If you want to hold them accountable for these commitments, you might ask participants to share them with the group.

Context

Servant-leaders are not stereotypical leaders. They know that by intentionally and consistently demonstrating a servant's attitude, they help create a culture of humility and servanthood that permeates the entire church.

Discussion

1. What is the biggest obstacle you face in developing an attitude of servanthood?
2. How do you avoid being perceived as someone who is "above" doing menial tasks?
3. What are some ways you can express an attitude of servanthood to others in our church?
4. What are some ways you can anonymously demonstrate servanthood outside our church?
5. What is the difference between being a servant and simply performing acts of service?

Activity 1

Fostering servanthood within your church requires conscious effort. Our human tendency is to think more highly of ourselves than of others and to avoid situations that require us to serve. To counteract this tendency, arrange an opportunity for you and your leadership team to perform an act of service as a group. Serve the homeless or others in need, for example.

Activity 2

Even acts of service can become means of attracting attention and inducing pride. One of the best

THE POWER OF E & P

Gaining support through education and participation

H ave you ever wondered why intelligent, loyal, normally happy team members don't readily accept organizational decisions that you or your close circle of confidants made behind closed doors? Even though they can't deny the logic behind a decision, the research supporting it, and the quality of the decision itself, the people you serve sometimes don't quickly embrace your ideas.

Many times these lukewarm responses are the result of inadequate education and participation. Think about it. In most problem-solving processes, a leader or leadership team spends a good deal of time gathering facts, getting feedback, and pondering possible solutions. Then the solution is announced, usually with very little explanation. The staff is given nothing close to the amount of information the leader or team examined before reaching a conclusion.

When people get the result without the process, they often ask excellent questions: "Was there a problem?" "Why was this decision made?" "Who was involved in the process?" "When did they get together?" These and other questions have more to do with the process by which the conclusion was reached than with the conclusion itself. By taking the time to summarize the decision-making process, leaders stand a much better chance of seeing those they lead reach the same conclusions within a short time.

When a decision directly affects people, as many leadership decisions do, they want to participate in it. Otherwise, they feel helpless and undervalued. The challenge for leaders is to gain input prior to making a decision without stirring the pot unnecessarily or giving the impression that the outcome will be the result of a popular vote. Obviously, some decisions should be made quietly by a few because vague, brief discussions among many can stir up sentiment against a necessary change. (A notorious example is selecting church carpet. Unfortunately, fights over flooring crop up all too frequently in the histories of many churches!) But leaders must carefully weigh the potential damage to feelings and team spirit if others are not included in at least initial discussions about possible solutions. Often they have legitimate input that should affect the outcome. Many times they just want affirmation that their opinions are important and were considered in the decision-making process.

Jesus spent substantial time with his disciples, teaching and discussing Kingdom principles. While he never compromised his principles, he did allow for adequate interaction with his team. Since none of us has anything close to Jesus' authority or credibility, it is even more important that we discuss leadership decisions if we

 THE POWER OF E & P

expect them to be accepted. Merely telling people about a decision won't induce ownership. Without ownership, a decision may be greeted by token support, action without passion, and even sabotage.

Leaders can usually avoid unnecessary fretting and resistance to their ideas by adjusting the process by which they make decisions. While it will require a bit more effort and time, the result will be far less costly.

THE POWER OF E & P

Gaining support through education and participation

Context

Little problems can balloon into huge issues when people feel they've been denied a voice in the decision-making process. People want to participate in decisions that affect them, and they want to be informed of the processes used to make decisions. Leaders who fail to educate and invite appropriate participation in decision-making will have difficulty convincing those they lead of the rightness of their decisions.

Discussion

1. Think of an example of a decision that directly affected you and was made without your input. How did you react?
2. Can you think of a situation in which simply explaining the rationale behind a decision cleared the air for concerned team members?
3. Think of a decision that was reached after those who would be affected by it were asked to participate. Did their participation result in a better decision as well as a sense of ownership?
4. Under what circumstances should participation not be invited in the decision-making process?
5. What are two to three situations in your area of responsibility that could benefit from better education and participation?

Activity 1

Before the lesson, but after everyone is settled, tell the group that you've decided to move the meeting to another location. As participants pick up their belongings, inform them of the new location. (Make sure the new meeting place is less comfortable and less appropriate than the place you usually use.) When you arrive at the new location, tell participants that all of your future meetings will be held there, and announce a change in future meeting times and even days. When you begin to hear negative feedback or at least sense some irritation, you will have created a setting for a teachable moment. Ask participants to use this experience to consider how others feel when they're informed of decisions without knowing the rationale behind them or without having been given the opportunity to participate in the decision-making process.

Activity 2

Ask team members to identify one ministry or church problem that must be faced. Then ask them to write down the names of people who should participate in developing a solution. Ask them to explore the risks of leaving certain people out of the loop. Finally, ask them to come up with an appropriate way to educate everyone affected by the solution.

leadership
movies

HOOSIERS

Dealing with power struggles with formal and informal leaders

Hoosiers is the story of an aging coach who comes to a small, rural, Indiana high school to lead the basketball team. As in many small communities and organizations, newcomers are seen as outsiders and are given the cold shoulder until they've proven themselves. The town thrives on basketball, and many of the town leaders have strong opinions about how the team should be coached. The new coach is equally tenacious and has a reputation for being a bit rough.

As you watch the film, consider these aspects from a leader's point of view: being new, breaking into existing power structures, and striving to create change. Make mental or written notes about what you learn about leading.

The following specific questions are designed to help you dissect the film's leadership lessons.

- Consider the roles, attitudes, and actions of

    the coach

    the principal

    the adult town leaders

    the adversarial female teacher

    the obstinate team players

    the positive team players

    the alcoholic assistant coach

- How are these characters representative of the various roles people play in churches? What can you learn from these characters?

- What is the most significant leadership principle that emerges from this movie?

- What other leadership principles did you glean from the film?

- Which leadership practices might fit in your organizational context, and which might not?

LESSON 46

HOOSIERS

Dealing with power struggles with formal and informal leaders

The big leadership theme of this film is the struggle for power. The coach was confronted by people whose methods were entrenched in tradition—a common problem in leadership. Obviously, every leadership struggle does not turn out as nicely as the one in this movie did, but if leaders are to prevail, they sometimes must do battle with those whose ideas are stuck in a "that's the way we've always done it" mentality.

After exploring the questions on the participants' page, discuss these:

- How did the coach take authority away from the informal leaders in the community?

- Who were some influencers who struggled to usurp the coach's power?

- How did the coach confront divisive team members?

- What were pivotal points at which power struggles came to a head?

- What mistakes do you think the coach made in gaining allies?

- What do you think the coach did well?

- What leadership role did the principal play?

- How did the coach prepare and discipline the team? Was he too hard or too soft?

- How did the coach inspire the team along the way?

- What do you think would have happened if the team had not won?

LESSON **47**

BRAVEHEART

A model of bravery, vision, and selfless leading

This is the inspiring story of Sir William Wallace, the leader of a rebellion in thirteenth-century Scotland. While some of the scenes depict brutal aspects of war, Wallace's story serves as a contemporary model for leaders who must confront evil, exude bravery, and cast vision.

The following questions are designed to help you dissect the film's leadership lessons.

- Wallace was personally involved in this struggle. How might the results have been different if he had led from a safe distance?

- Who were the key influencers in this movie? How did their approaches to leading differ?

- How did Wallace's resistance to seeking personal power tend to work for him rather than against him?

- How did Wallace stand up against those who would compromise their values for personal gain?

- The film depicts betrayal. Who betrayed whom? How do you feel and respond when betrayed?

- What one big leadership principle emerges from this film?

- What concepts from this movie can you transfer to your specific leadership situation?

OK TO COPY

LESSON 47

BRAVEHEART

A model of bravery, vision, and selfless leading

In the face of the compromise, self-aggrandizement, and lack of commitment that are all too common among leaders today, this film demonstrates the motivational power of a courageous, selfless leader who fights for the benefit of the people.

The movie lives up to its R rating, primarily due to its violent but realistic depictions of medieval warfare. There is also a subtle theme of immorality in one or two scenes and some naked male rumps during a comical battle scene. If these elements are not a deterrent to your selection of the movie, you'll find a predominantly inspirational movie about leadership.

After exploring the questions on the participants' page, discuss these:

- One of the king's sons is portrayed as weak and fearful. What is the difference between the informal influence of Wallace and the positional authority of the king's son?

- How did events in Wallace's past affect his involvement in leadership?

- The scene in which Wallace rallies the troops before a major battle depicts a powerful example of vision-casting. Note the difference between those who cast doubts and Wallace, who exudes hope and inspiration. (Because this is a compelling scene, you may want to replay it in conjunction with the discussion.)

- While Wallace and his forces won some victories, they also suffered defeats. How does a leader weigh the costs? How did Wallace decide whether to quit or go forward?

- Some of Wallace's victories came through strategic preparation and creative ideas, thinking outside the military box. What are some examples of these? How does this relate to modern-day organizational effectiveness?

LESSON **48**

CRIMSON TIDE

New and old styles of leading under pressure

The setting of *Crimson Tide* is a submarine. Incomplete data causes a conflict between the commanding officer and his executive officer. Should they obey their original orders and launch a nuclear warhead, or should they wait in light of an incomplete, unclear message that was received after the original orders? This is a classic military depiction of the friction that arises between old and new leadership mind-sets. The old approach is more dominant, autocratic, and top-down. The new approach is more thoughtful, participative, and oriented toward information gathering. While at times the language in this film is rough, the comparison between old and new leadership styles is well worth viewing.

The following specific questions are designed to help you dissect the film's leadership lessons.

- Why was incomplete information dangerous in this movie? Why is it dangerous in any church?

- What do you do when policy and protocol get in the way of making a decision, or when they lead to wrong decisions that can cause great damage?

- Who were the two leaders, and how would you describe the attitude, philosophy, and style of each?

- Which servicemen played pivotal roles in the outcome? Why?

- Who was right in the end?

- What major leadership lesson did you glean from this movie?

- What leadership concepts can you transfer to your professional life?

OK TO COPY

LESSON 48

CRIMSON TIDE

New and old styles of leading under pressure

This military movie is based upon a true story. The harsh military language may make it unacceptable for certain participants, and there is some violence. However, both the language and the violence seem appropriate to the context; they are not used gratuitously. This movie is an excellent depiction of the friction that arises between leaders of the old school and those of the new.

After exploring the questions on the participants' page, discuss these:

• How do you respond in a confrontation with another leader or influencer who disagrees with your decisions?

• In the film, how did each leader's allies affect the dynamics and outcome?

• In this conflict, both the commanding officer and the executive officer needed a good understanding of the systems, resources, and staff. How does their need to know relate to contemporary organizational life?

• What were elements that made these conditions so critical (such as limited information, inability to communicate, protocol systems, short time deadline, gravity of the possible outcomes)?

• Both leaders were unwilling to back down, even after exhaustively arguing the point. How did each strive to obtain more power in order to win?

• Whose leadership style was best? In what ways were both effective?

• What if the commanding officer had been right? How would this have changed the ending?

BABE

Using people skills instead of coercion to lead

At first, you may not think this comical family movie offers much in the way of leadership insights. But this film has several components that make it a good leadership film as well as feel-good entertainment. It's about a pig who is fortunate enough to avoid the slaughterhouse and is raised by a farmer's dogs. The pig, Babe, begins to think he is a sheepdog. His approach to leading the sheep is different from his mentor's, but he turns out to be much more effective.

The following specific questions are designed to help you dissect the film's leadership lessons.

• If the male sheepdog represented the old style of leading, what did you learn about it?

• What roles did some of the other characters (the sheep, the farmer, his wife, the duck, and the mother dog) play in Babe's life?

• How did Babe's upbringing affect how he eventually learned to lead?

• How did Babe's relationship with the sheep eventually become an important leadership tool?

• What did the male sheepdog think about sheep, and how did this affect his attempts to influence them?

• What is the main leadership point in this film?

• What leadership concepts can you transfer to your area of responsibility?

OK TO COPY

LESSON 49

BABE

Using people skills instead of coercion to lead

This is a great study in leadership for those who prefer to steer clear of the language and violence of *Braveheart* and *Crimson Tide*. It's also a great film to watch with children. The theme is leadership styles. The male sheepdog models a twentieth-century, industrial age, top-down, autocratic approach to leadership, while the pig reflects a twenty-first century style of leadership characterized by kinder, gentler, team-oriented, more communicative, and appreciative methods.

After exploring the questions on the participants' page, discuss these:

- How did the sheep respond to the sheepdog's approach to leading?

- The dog gets results, but is that all that's necessary in leading? (Notice how boldly the dog justifies and explains his views.)

- What role does the farmer play in believing in and preparing the pig to herd sheep?

- How does the mother dog help the pig?

- Why are others important in the life of a leader, especially in his or her formative years?

- The pig is far from perfect, yet he emerges as a successful influencer. How can this encourage leaders?

- Why is it important to understand and get close to those we seek to lead?

- How is the pig's grateful attitude exemplary of a servant-leader?

- Which of this film's leadership principles might be important to your area of responsibility?

50

TUCKER

Entrepreneurial leadership and the power of perseverance

Tucker is based on a true story about an entrepreneur who has an idea for a better car. Through passion, perseverance, and creativity, Tucker develops a revolutionary car that intimidates the giant auto manufacturers. This movie deals with entrepreneurial leadership and shows what it takes to develop any new idea. It shows that there are no guarantees that innovations will see the light of day and that, if they do, determined leadership will more than likely be the driving force behind them.

The following specific questions are designed to help you dissect the film's leadership lessons.

• How did the idea person (Tucker) and the engineer resolve their disagreements? (Hint: The *what* must always precede the *how*.)

• What steps were required to take a raw idea from its conception to the showroom?

• What challenges arose from building the new car?

• How did Tucker handle setbacks?

• Did he ultimately win? Why or why not?

• In light of this movie, explain the statement, "Resources flow to ideas."

• What significant leadership principle did you glean from this movie?

• Which of the film's leadership concepts can you transfer to your own situation?

LESSON 50

TUCKER

*Entrepreneurial leadership and
the power of perseverance*

Resiliency and refusing to take no for an answer are the leadership themes of this film. Effective leaders have a can-do attitude toward their goals, and this tends to be contagious. Even though Tucker's innovation was never mass-produced, the process of getting the car to market in spite of huge challenges is a template for determined leaders today.

After exploring the questions on the participants' page, discuss these:

• Discuss the dynamic tension that nearly always exists between "idea people" and the "how-to" people.

• For an idea to survive, why must you begin with the *must* do rather than the *how* to? Why are both sides necessary?

• How did Tucker select his team members? How is this important to leadership?

• Identify at least two seemingly insurmountable roadblocks Tucker faced. How did he overcome them? How does this relate to our church?

• How can successful new ideas threaten powerful people?

• "The one with the most power wins, not the one who is right." Discuss this statement in light of the fact that the big auto manufacturers prevented Tucker from mass-producing his car.

• Discuss Tucker's energy and can-do attitude. How can leaders today use the same traits to get things done?

Flagship church resources

from Group Publishing

Innovations From Leading Churches

Flagship Church Resources are your shortcut to innovative and effective leadership ideas. You'll find ideas for every area of church leadership, including pastoral ministry, adult ministry, youth ministry, and children's ministry.

Flagship Church Resources are created by the leaders of thriving, dynamic, and trend-setting churches around the country. These nationally recognized teaching churches host regional leadership conferences and are respected by other pastors and church leaders because their approaches to ministry are so effective. These flagship church resources reveal the proven ideas, programs, and principles that these churches have put into practice.

Flagship Church Resources currently available:

- *60 Simple Secrets Every Pastor Should Know*
- *The Perfectly Imperfect Church: Redefining the "Ideal Church"*
- *The Winning Spirit: Empowering Teenagers Through God's Grace*
- *Ultimate Skits: 20 Parables for Driving Home Your Point*
- *Doing Life With God: Real Stories Written by Students*
- *Doing Life With God 2: Real Stories Written by Students*
- *The Visual Edge: Compelling Video Connectors for Your Worship Experience*
- *Mission-Driven Worship: Helping Your Changing Church Celebrate God*
- *An Unstoppable Force: Daring to Become the Church God Had in Mind*
- *A Follower's Life: 12 Group Studies On What It Means to Walk With Jesus*
- *Leadership Essentials for Children's Ministry*
- *Keeping Your Head Above Water:*
  Refreshing Insights for Church Leadership
- *Seeing Beyond Church Walls: Action Plans for Touching Your Community*
- *unLearning Church:*
  Just When You Thought You Had Leadership all Figured Out!
- *Morph!: The Texture of Leadership for Tomorrow's Church*
- *The Quest for Christ: Discipling Today's Young Adults*
- *LeadingIdeas: To-the-Point Training for Christian Leaders*
- *Igniting Passion in Your Church: Becoming Intimate with Christ*
- *No More Lone Rangers: How to Build a Team-Centered Youth Ministry*

With more to follow!